Positive Thinking for a Successful Life

Build Your Business

By

Cole Dylan Mundo

Table Of Contents

Inter-company training is a good way to achieve stable growth. Employee preparation will concentrate on the company's needs, rather than what's beyond the company. Through a holistic training strategy, a deep framework can be developed that allows workers to concentrate and work towards goals. Training promotes growth changes when workers know what is expected of them in the company's broader context, enabling them to continue to work efficiently even as the individual aspects of their employment shift. Training instills a sense of career in people expecting to continue and develop with the business. Training helps the mindsets of workers to be adapted to that of the business community, making them ideally suited to the business.

Introduction

Don't believe anything. It doesn't matter where you read it or who said it, even if I said it because it coincides with your purpose and common sense.

Buddha

Everyone learns differently, so you certainly know the best way to learn. You may want to read this book once to get a sense of the overall process before you start the work of building the life you desire; the concepts are presented in an order that makes one on the other.

There are hundreds of books have been written about what it takes to be successful in the industry, and a thousand more about achieving success in life. With such a broad topic, and with so many things that can play a role in making us happy, it can be challenging to narrow it down to a shortlist of items that someone can read and apply in their lives.

But across those thousands of books and papers, among the plethora of legends and tales, you'll find some common themes that have been woven throughout. You will discover ideas about us as human beings that many of us care about, but never strive hard enough to achieve. You will learn about values and choices that we all wish we could adhere to but still fail to grasp. Here are some of the stuff you're going to find among the stories of those who have experienced success in business (and in life)-which ones do you already have and which do you need to get?

You can find that you already know some of the values here. That's great! But ask yourself, am I doing it? If not, make a promise to bring them into action — now!

You can find yourself resisting taking any of the actions suggested. But my experience has shown that the ones you fight the most are the ones you need to accept the most. Know, reading this book is not the same as doing a task, no more than reading a weight loss book is the same as only eating fewer calories and doing more.

1

The Fundamentals of Success

You will take personal responsibility. You can't change the circumstances, the seasons, or the climate, but you can change yourself.

Jim Rohm

1.1 Take 100% Responsibility for Your Life

One of the most pervasive misconceptions in our society today is that we are entitled to a great life — that somehow, somewhere, someone (certainly not us) is responsible for filling our lives with continuous joy, exciting career choices, and maintaining the time of family.

But the real truth — and the one lesson of this entire book — is that there is only one person responsible for the quality of life you enjoy. That person is you, man.

If you desire to be successful, you have to take 100% responsibility for all you've done in your life. This includes the level of your accomplishments, the results you generate, the nature of your relationships, the state of your health and fitness, your wages, your debts, your feelings — everything!

• You Have to Give Up All Your Excuses

A chemist who has invented more than 325 uses for peanuts if you want to build the life of your dreams, then you will also have to take 100% responsibility for your life.

This means giving up all of your excuses, all of your victim's accounts, all of the reasons why you can't and why you haven't been up till now, and all of your responsibility for outside circumstances. You've got to give them all up forever. You have to take the stance that you've always had the power to make something different, to get it right, to achieve the desired result. For whatever reason — ignorance, lack of knowledge, fear, need to be light, need to feel safe — you choose not to exercise the strength. Who knows why that is? This doesn't matter to you.

The past has been the past. All that matters are present that from this point on, you choose — what's right, it's a choice — you choose to behave as though (that's all you need — to behave as if) you're 100% responsible for all that's going on or doesn't happen to you.

When something doesn't work out as expected, you're going to ask yourself, "how did I make it? What did I think? What were my convictions, huh? What have I said or not said? What have I done or not done to produce the result? How did I get the other person to behave like that? What do I need to do differently next time I get the result I want? "a very basic but very relevant formula that will make this principle of 100% accountability even clearer to you. The formula is:

$E + R = O$ *(Event + Reaction = Outcome)*

The basic concept is that any outcome you encounter in your life (whether it is success or failure, prosperity or deprivation, health or disease, intimacy or separation, happiness or frustration) is the product of how you react to an earlier event or event in your life.

• What You Experience Now Is the Result of The Decisions You Have Made in The Past

All you experience in life — both internally and externally — is the result of how you have reacted to a previous case.

You only have power over three things in your life — the thoughts you think about, the images you imagine, and the actions you take (your behavior). How you use these three factors decides what you're feeling. If you don't like what you're doing and experiencing, you've got to change your reactions. Shift the negative to positive feelings. Adjust what you're dreaming of. Adjust your habits, please. Adjust what you've read. Please update your mates. Change the way you talk.

• You Have to Give Up Blaming

You can never be successful as long as you continue to blame someone or something else for your lack of success. If you're going to be a winner, you have to realize the truth — you're the one that took the initiative, thought the emotions, produced the feelings and made the decisions that brought you to where you are now. It was you, man!

• You have to give up the complaining

You have to assume that something better exists to complain about something or anything. You need to have a reference point for something that you choose not to be able to take responsibility for making. Let's take a closer look at that.

If you didn't believe that there was anything better — more income, a larger home, a more fulfilling career, more fun, a more caring spouse — you couldn't complain. So, you've got this vision of something better, and you know you'd prefer it, but you're not willing to take the chances that would be needed to build it.

1.2 Be Sure Why You Are Here

Every one of us is born with a life purpose. Identifying, re-membering, and upholding this intent is probably the most important action that effective people take. They take the time to realize what they're here to do — and then they do it with zeal and excitement.

• What Have You Been Put on This Planet to Do?

You see, it's easy to get sidetracked on your life's path without a purpose in life. It's easy to wander and float to accomplish a little.

But with a reason, everything in life seems to be falling into place. Being "on purpose" means doing what you want to do, doing what you're good at, and doing what's important to you.

Decide on your key goal in life, and then plan all your activities around it.

Brian Tracy

If you know what your life's mission is, you will plan all your activities around it. Anything you're doing should be an ex-pression of your intent. If that formula doesn't suit an opera-tion, you wouldn't be working on it.

• What's The "Why" Behind Everything you're Doing?

Without the purpose of directing you as a guide, your goals and action plans cannot ultimately satisfy you. You don't want to get to the top of the ladder only to find out that you had it leaning against the wrong wall.

The good news is that you don't have to go abroad to get away from the day-to-day demands of your life long enough to build space to explore what you're here to do. You may simply take the time to complete two simple exercises that will help you to explain your intent.

• Staying on Purpose

Once you have decided and written down the meaning of your life, read it every day, preferably in the morning. If you are creative or highly visual, you may want to draw or paint a symbol or image that reflects your life purpose and then hang it somewhere (in the refrigerator, opposite your office, by your bed) where you see it every day. This is going to keep you focused on your goal.

1.3 Determine What You Want

The first important step to get something out of life is this: decide what you want.

Ben stein

Once you've decided why you're here, you will decide what to do, be, and have. What is to accomplish? Who you want to experience? And what things will you acquire? You have to determine where you want to be on the journey from where you are. In other words, what do you see as success?

One of the biggest reasons people don't get what they want is they didn't know what they want. They haven't described their desires in explicit detail.

• Early Childhood Training Gets into The Way of What

You wish to the inside of each of us is the tiny "you" seed you were supposed to become. Unfortunately, in answer to your parents, teachers, coaches, and other role models of adults, you may have buried this seed.

And what's happened? Someone on the way said:

Don't touch that!;

Stay away from it;

Keep your hands off;

Stop what you're doing, do what I want you to do!;

• Don't Live Someone Else's Dreams

After several years of these prohibitions, most of us gradually lost contact with our bodies' needs and hearts' desires and somehow kept trying to find out what other people expected us to do. We learned to act and to gain approval. As a result, we do a lot of things we don't want to do now, but satisfy a lot of others:

- We go to medical school because that's what dad wanted for us, wedding to honor our mother, instead of following our dream arts career, we get "true work", we go straight to graduate school instead of a year off and backpacking around Europe.

And how do you and your true passions reclaim? How do you get back to what you want, without doubt, shame, or inhibition? How can you reconnect with your love?

Starting at the smallest point, you respect your interests in any situation — no matter how big or small. Don't think they're tiny. They might be incompatible with anyone else, but they're not yours.

• Avoid Settling for Less Than You Deserve

If you're going to exert your leverage to get what you want out of existence, you'll have to quit saying, "I don't know; I don't care; it doesn't matter to me "— or the new teen favorite," whatever. "When you're presented with a decision, no matter how tiny or insignificant, behave as though you're preferred. Ask yourself, if I did, what'd it be? If I cared, who'd I prefer? If it mattered, what would I do?

Not being clear about what you want and making the needs and interests of others more important than yours is simply a habit.

• Make an "I Want" List

One of the best ways to start clarifying what you want is to list 30 things you want to do, 30 things you want to have, and 30 things you want to be before you die. It's a perfect way to roll the ball.

However, the real thing you start dreaming about after the 15-minute exercise ends: "I want people to love me. I want to express myself. I want a difference. I want to feel strong, "that's true expressions of your core values.

• Clarify the Dream of Your Perfect Life

This book's theme is how to get to where you want to be. To do this, you will learn two things — where you are and where you want to go. Your dream is a comprehensive overview of your goal. It explains in detail what your destination looks like. Your vision will include the following seven areas to build a healthy and productive life: work and job, income, leisure and free time, health and wellness, relationships, personal interests, and commitment to the wider community.

At this point in the trip, you don't need to learn exactly how to get there. All that's necessary is to find out where. If you explain what, how will you be taken care of?

1.4 Believe It's Possible

Napoleon hill once said, "whatever the mind can imagine and believe, it can achieve." actually, the mind is such a potent instrument; it can produce whatever you want. Yet it's easy to believe what you want.

• You Get What You Expect

Scientists used to assume that humans responded to knowledge coming from outside the brain. But today, instead of learning to adapt to what the brain expects to happen next, based on previous experience.

How does the brain do this? Neuropsychologists who research the theory of anticipation claim that we spend all our lives being conditioned. Across skills worth a lifetime, our brain ultimately learns what to do next — whether or not it inevitably happens. And when our brain expects anything to happen, we always do just what we expected.

Therefore, keeping positive expectations in your mind is so necessary. When you replace your old negative thoughts with more positive ones — when you start believing that what you want is possible — your brain will finally take over the job of doing that for you. The mind will simply hope to achieve that result.

Believe in and go for it, sooner or later, those who win are those who believe they can.

1.5 Trust Yourself

You weren't an accident. You're not mass-produced. You're not an assembly line commodity. The master craftsman carefully designed, expressly created, and lovingly put you on earth.

Max Lucado

If you are going to succeed in building your dream life, you have to believe you can make it happen. You will find you have the right stuff to pull it off. You must believe in yourself. If you name it self-esteem, self-confidence, or self-assurance, it's a deep-seated conviction you have what it takes — the skills, inner power, strengths, and skills to achieve the desired outcomes.

• Believing in Yourself Is an Attitude

It's an attitude you've built over time. While it helps if you had optimistic and loving parents, the truth is that most of us had run-of-the-mill parents who unwittingly passed on the same limiting values and negative conditioning with which they grew up.

If you believe for yourself and behave as if it's true, then you'll do the stuff you need to get the result. If you think it's hard, you won't do what's required and you won't deliver the result. It's a self-fulfilling prophecy.

• You Have to Give Up, "I Can't"

If you want success, you have to give up the expression "I can't," and all its cousins, including "I wish I could." I can't disempower you. They make you weaker when you say them. Your brain is programmed to solve every problem and achieve your target. The words you think and utter affect your body. We see that in youth. When you were a child, you didn't pause. You thought you could climb something. No barrier was too high to try to conquer. Yet little by little, your sense of invincibility is influenced by the emotional and physical violence you endure from your relatives, peers, and teachers before you believe you can.

• What Others Think Is Not Your Responsibility

If making others trust in you and your vision was a prerequisite for success, most of us will never succeed. You need to base your decisions on your objectives and desires — not the ambitions, expectations, views, and assumptions of your parents, friends, spouse, kids, and coworkers. Stop thinking about other people and follow your heart.

• Dr. Daniel Ameen's 18/40/60 Rule:

When you're 18, you're concerned about what everyone's thinking of you; when you're 40, you don't give a damn what anyone thinks of you; when you're 60, you know nobody's thinking of you.

Surprise, amazement! Most of the time, nobody thinks about you! They're too busy worried about their own lives, and if they think about you, they're wondering what you're feeling about them. People speak about themselves, not you. Think about it — every time you're concerned about what other people think about your plans, aspirations, clothing, hair, and home, it could all be better spent thinking about and doing things that will accomplish your goals.

1.6 Become an Inverse Paranoid

I've always been a paranoid opposite. I act like everybody's part of a conspiracy to boost my well-being.

Stan Dale

W. Clement stone was once identified as paranoid. Instead of thinking the world intended to hurt him, he wanted to believe the world was planning to do him well. Instead of seeing any problematic or frustrating experience as unfavorable, he saw it as something that was intended to enrich him, inspire him, or advance his causes.

• What unbelievably optimistic confidence!

Imagine how easy it would be if you were always expecting the world to help you and giving you an opportunity. Productive people do that.

The earlier and more often, you start looking for the positive. And if you take the mentality it's coming, the less frustrated and depressed you'll be while you're waiting.

• Look for the Opportunity in All

What if you welcome every encounter in your life with the question "what is the future opportunity this is?" The super-successful approach every encounter as an opportunity. They join every conversation with the hope of something positive coming from it. And they know what they'll find and predict.

When you take the view that "good" is not an accident — that for a cause everyone and all that happens in your life is there — and that the universe pushes you toward your ultimate destiny for learning, progress, and achievement, you will begin to see every event was an opportunity for improvement and progression in your life.

Create a tiny sign or poster with words on what the occasion is? And put it on your desk or your tablet, so you'll be continuously encouraged to look for the positive in any case.

1.7 Unleash Goal-Setting Power

When you want to be happy, set your target, unleash your strength, and promote your hopes.

Andrew Carnegie

Once you know your life objective, define your dream, and explain what your exact needs and aspirations are, you will turn them into concrete, tangible goals and priorities and then act on them with the assurance that you will achieve them.

Experts know that the brain is a goal-seeking organism. Whatever target you offer your subconscious mind; it will work night and day.

• How Much, When?

To ensure a target unleashes your subconscious mind's strength, it must meet two criteria. It must be mentioned that you and everyone else can calculate it. I'll lose 10 pounds is not as strong as I'll weigh 135 pounds on June 30 at 5 pm. The second is better because on June 30, at 5 o'clock, everyone will turn up and look at your scale. Either 135pounds or less or not. Note that both parameters are how much (some substantial amount such as words, pounds, dollars, square feet, or points) and when (specific time and date).

Be as precise as possible with all aspects of your goals — including make, model, color, year, and height, weight, form, form, and other specifics. Know, vague targets yield loosely.

• You Need Goals That Stretch You

When you build your goals, make sure to write down some major ones that will stretch you. It pays to have goals that will allow you to evolve. It's nice to have some ambitions that make you uncomfortable. Why? Why? Since the ultimate aim, besides achieving your material objectives, is to become a life master. And you'll need to learn new skills to do so, develop your view of what's possible, create new relationships, and learn to resolve your doubts, worries, and roadblocks.

• Make A Goals Book

Another essential way to improve your goals is to develop a goals book. Purchase a three-ring binder, scrapbook, or 81/2" journal. Develop a separate page for each purpose. Write the goal at the top of the page and then illustrate it with images, sentences, and phrases you cut out from newspapers, catalogs, and travel brochures that represent your goal as you have already accomplished.

As new ambitions and aspirations surface, just add them to your list and target book. Check your target book pages regularly.

Keep your most important goal in your pocket

Write down your most important objective at all times on the back of my business card. Every time you open your wallet, remember your most important goal.

Considerations, Worries, and Roadblocks

It's essential to realize that when you set a goal, three obstacles can arise that hinder most people — but not you. If you know these three things are part of the process, then you can view them as what they are — just stuff to handle — instead of preventing them.

Such three barriers are concerns, doubts, and roadblocks

1.8 Chunk It Down

The secret of getting ahead is getting underway. The secret of getting started is to break your complex, overwhelming tasks into small, manageable tasks, and then start with the first.

Mark twain

Our most important life goals already sound too daunting. We never see them as a collection of small, workable tasks, but breaking down a massive target into smaller goals — and accomplishing them one at a time — is precisely how to achieve any big goal. So, after you have decided what you want and set measurable targets with specific deadlines, the next step is to determine all the individual action steps that you will need to take to achieve your goal.

• How to Chunk It Down?

There are several ways to figure out what action you will need to take to resolve any purpose. One is talking with people who have already done what you want to do and see what steps they have taken. They will give you all the required steps from their experience, as well as advice on what pitfalls to avoid. Another way is to buy a book or manual which describes the process. Starting from the end is another way, and looking back. You just turn a blind eye and picture the future is now, and that you have already achieved your goal. Then just look back and see what you've had to do to get to where you are now. What was the last thing you did? And then the idea before, and then the word back before you get to the first action with which you had to begin.

Remember, it's all right not to know how to do something. It's all right to ask for guidance and advice from those who know. Sometimes you can get it for free, and sometimes you've got to pay for it. Get used to asking, keep researching and asking until you can create a realistic action plan that will get you from where you're going to where you want to go.

A valuable technique for creating an action plan for your objectives is called mind mapping.

• Use Mind Mapping

Mind mapping is a simple but powerful procedure to create a detailed list of tasks to achieve your goal. It lets you determine what information you're going to need to gather, who you're going to need to talk to, what small steps you're going to need to take, how much money you're going to need to earn or raise, what deadlines you're going to have to meet, and so on — for every goal.

• Next, Make a Daily To-Do List

After you've completed a mind map for your target, turn all the to-do items into everyday action items by listing each item on your daily to-do list, and setting a date for each item to complete.

Then arrange them in the correct order into your calendar and do whatever it takes to remain on track.

Do first Things first

To remain on track and comply with the essential item. When you do your toughest job early in the day, it sets the tone for the rest of your day. It creates momentum and builds your trust, both of which move you further and faster towards your goal.

• Plan Your Day A Night Before

One of the most potent high-achieving tools used to bump things down, gain control of their lives, and increase their productivity is to plan their next day the night before. There are two main reasons why this is such a powerful strategy for success:

1. If you plan your day the night before — making a to-do list and spending a few minutes visualizing exactly how you want the day to go — your subconscious mind will be working on these tasks all night long. It's going to think about creative ways to solve any problem, overcome any obstacle, and achieve your desired outcomes. And if we can believe some of the newer theories of quantum physics, it will also send out waves of energy that will attract people and resources to you that you need to help achieve your goals.

2. You can start your day running by creating your to-do list the night before. You know precisely what you're going to do and in what order, and you've already put all the materials you need together. If you have five phone calls to make, you'd have them wrote down in the order you plan to make, with the phone numbers next to the name of the person and all the support materials at hand. By midmorning, you'd be way ahead of most people who waste the first half-hour of the day clearing their desk, making lists, finding the necessary paper-work — in short, and just getting ready to work.

• Use the Achiever's Focusing System

A valuable tool that will keep you focused on achieving all of your goals in the seven areas that we explained in your vision is the achiever's focusing system. It's a form that you can use to plan and hold yourself accountable for 13 weeks of goals and action.

1.9 Success Leaves Clues

One of the best things about living in today's world of wealth and prosperity is that almost anything you want to do was achieved by someone else already. Whether it is losing weight, starting a company, being financially stable, winning breast cancer or hosting a perfect dinner party, it doesn't matter — someone has already done it and left clues in the form of books, manuals, audio and video programs, university classes, online courses, seminars, and workshops.

• Who Did What You Wanted to Do?

There are several books and courses on how to do it for virtu-ally everything you want to do. Better yet, just phone calls away are people who have already successfully done what you want to do and are available as teachers, facilitators, men-tors, counselors, coaches, and consultants.

When you take advantage of this information, you will discover that life is simply a connect-to-dot game and that all the dots have already been identified and organized by someone else. Follow the blueprint, use the system, or work the program they provide

• Why People Don't Seek Out Clues

You most likely thought about approaching an expert for advice but rejected the idea with thoughts like why would someone take the time to tell me what they were doing? Why would they teach me and create a competition of their own? Banish your thoughts. You're going to find that most people love to talk about how they built their business or accomplished their goals.

Unfortunately, however, most of us do not take advantage of all the resources available to us. There are several reasons why we don't: it never happens to us; it's inconvenient, though; connecting dots means hard work, and honestly, most people don't want to work that hard.

• Seek Out for the Clues

Here are three ways you can start searching for clues:

1. Seek a teacher, coach, mentor; a manual, book, or audio program; or an internet resource to help you achieve one of your key objectives.

2. Look for a person who has already done what you wanted to do, and ask the person if you can talk to him or her for half an hour about how best to proceed.

3. Ask someone if you're going to follow them for an entire day and watch them work. Or simply offer to be a volunteer, assistant, or intern to someone you think you can learn from.

1.10 Release the Brakes

Everything you want is outside your comfort zone.

Robert Allen

Most people are driving their psychological emergency brakes through their lives. They hold on to negative images of themselves or suffer the effects of compelling experiences that have not yet been released. They're staying in a comfort zone entirely of their own making. They possess false views about fact or harbor shame and self-doubt. And these misleading thoughts and pre-programmed comfort environments often balance out their positive intentions as they attempt to accomplish their goals — no matter how hard they try.

On the other hand, successful individuals have discovered that instead of using greater willpower as the motor to propel their performance, it is easily better to "release the brakes" by letting go of their narrow values and modifying their self-images.

• Get Out of Your Comfort Zone

Your comfort zone as a prison in which you live — a largely self-created prison. It consists of a collection of cants, musts, musts, musts, and other unfounded beliefs formed by all the negative thoughts and decisions that you have accumulated and reinforced in your lifetime. You might even have been trained to limit yourself.

• Stop Re-Creating the Same Over and Over Experience!

An essential concept that successful people understand is that you're never stuck. All you have to do is recreate the same experience over and over by thinking the same thoughts, maintaining the same beliefs, speaking the same words, and doing the same things.

Too often, we get stuck in an endless loop of reinforcement, which keeps us stuck in a constant downward spiral. Our limited thoughts create images in our minds, and those images govern the behavior of the governor, which in turn reinforces that limiting belief. As long as you keep complaining about your present circumstances, your mind is going to focus on it. By continually talking about, thinking about, and writing about the way things are, you are continually reinforcing the very same neural pathways in your brain that have brought you to where you are today. And you are regularly sending out the same vibrations that will continue to attract the same people and circumstances that you have already created.

Instead, to change this cycle, you must focus on thinking, talking, and writing about the reality that you want to create. You have to flood your unconscious with the thoughts and images of this new reality.

• Change Your Self-Talk with Affirmations

One way to expand your convenience field is to flood your subconscious mind with new ideas and pictures-a big bank account, a safe and trim body, fun jobs, fascinating friends, a memorable holiday-all of which have been your dreams. The strategy that you use is called affirmations. A statement is a declaration defining a target already achieved, such as "I love watching the sunset from the lanai of my beautiful beachfront condo on the Kaanapali coast of Maui" or "I enjoy feeling light and alive with my ideal body weight of thirty-five."

• How to Use Affirmations and Visualization?

1. Check your statements one to three times a day. The best periods are first in the morning, in the middle of the day, and during bed.

2. Read every statement loud, if necessary.

3. Close your eyes and see yourself as defined in the sentence. See it as if you were watching the scene from inside. In other words, don't see yourself in the picture; look at the situation as if you were living it.

4. Hear the sounds you may hear if you do what your argument describes adequately – the sound of waves, the noise of the crowd, and the national anthem. Include other famous people in your life who congratulate you and how pleased you are with your performance.

5. Know the emotions you will get when you succeed. The higher the sensations, the higher the process. (if you have trouble generating emotions, you might affirm that "I enjoy producing powerful feelings with affirmations easily in my successful work.")

6. Say your statement again and then repeat with the following statement this process.

2

Transform Yourself for Success

The most significant breakthrough of our century is the realisation that human beings can alter the outer aspects of their lives by changing the inner attitudes of their minds.

William James

2.1 Acknowledge the Productive Experience

Most people in our society think more of their mistakes than their achievements. It is the product of the "leave me alone — zap me" approach to parenting, teaching, and management that is so prevalent in our society.

When you were a child, your parents left you alone while you played and cooperated, and then zapped you while you made too much noise, became a nuisance, or were in trouble.

You probably got a perfunctory "nice job" when you got a's, but you got a significant lecture when you got c's and d's, or, heaven forbid, f. In training, most of the teachers marked the answers you got wrong with an x rather than the ones you got correct with a checkmark or a star. In sports, you were crying when you lost soccer or baseball. There was an almost always more emotional commitment to your errors, errors, and defeats than to your achievements.

Since the brain most readily recalls experiences that were followed by intense feelings, most people underestimate and underestimate the number of results they have had in comparison to the number of mistakes they have had. One way to combat this trend is to reflect on and celebrate your achievements actively. The sad reality is that we all have a lot more successes than failures — it's just that we set the bar too high for what we call progress.

• Start with Nine Major Successes

Here's an easy way to start an inventory of your significant accomplishments. Start by splitting your life into three equal periods — for example, if you are 45 years old, the three periods of time will be from birth to 15, 16 to 30, and 31 to 45. Then list the three achievements that you've had with each period.

• Can You List 100 Successes?

To further persuade yourself that you are the right person who will continue to do amazing things, complete the next phase of this exercise, and list 100 or more of your life achievements.

Depending on your age, you will also need to write down "passed first grade, passed second grade, passed third grade," but that's all right. The target is to get to 100.

• Build a Victory Log

Another essential way to keep adding poker chips to the stack is to keep a written record of your achievements. It can be as easy as running a list on a spiral-bound notebook or a folder on your screen, or it can be as complicated as a leather-bound journal. By remembering and writing down your achievements every day, you log them into your long-term memory, which boosts your self-esteem and strengthens your self-confidence. And later, if you need a boost in confidence, you can read back what you've posted.

Begin your victory log as soon as you can. You can also embellish it as a scrapbook with prints, awards, notes, and other reminders of your performance.

• Show Your Performance Symbols

Many researchers have discovered that what you see in your world has a psychological effect on your moods, attitudes, and actions. Your atmosphere has a great deal of impact on you. But here's an even more significant fact: you have almost complete control of your immediate environment. You can select which photographs are hung on your bedroom or office wall, what memorabilia is taped to your refrigerator or locker door, and what souvenirs you put on your desk or your workbench.

A successful strategy that helps improve your self-esteem and motivates you to achieve greater success in the future is the practice of surrounding yourself with rewards, images, and other items that remind you of your achievements. This could include medals from the days of the armed forces, a snapshot of your winning touchdown, your wedding photo, a plaque, a framed copy of the poem you wrote in the local newspaper, a letter of appreciation, your college certificate, or your eagle scout badger girl scout gold award.

• Reward the Inner Child

Within all of us, three distinct and different ego states work together to make up our personalities. We have a parent-like ego, an adult ego, and a child-like ego that behaves the same way parents, adults, and children do in real life.

As the parent of this "inner boy," one of your most important tasks is to invest in it and praise it for behaving on its own while you're doing your job.

A big part of achieving more success in your life is rewarding you when you excel. Paying yourself for your accomplishments keeps your inner child happy and obedient the next time it has to act. It knows that you can believe that you can finally deliver on your promises. When you don't, much like the areal kid, you'll start sabotaging your efforts by doing things like getting sick, having injuries, or making mistakes that cost you a promotion or even a career, and you'll be forced to take some time off. And that's only going to drive you further away from the performance you want.

2.2 Keep Your Eye on the Target

Successful people have a good outlook on life, no matter what's going on around them. They stay focused on their past achievements rather than their past mistakes, and on the next course in action that they need to take to get them closer to the accomplishment in their goals rather than to all the other challenges that life brings to them. They are also diligent in achieving their chosen objectives.

• The Daily Success Focus Journal

Another vital resource to keep your mind on the positive and your eye on the prize is the daily success mind journal. If you do this exercise regularly, you will increase your self-confidence and boost your success in all aspects of your life.

Just describe the five items you did during the day. You can be in any field of your life — work, education, family, faith, finance, wellness, personal growth, or community service.

Create a new version of the form then, once you have identified an accomplishment, write it down in the first box under "accomplishment." then, consider why that achievement is significant to you and write the explanation down in the second box under the heading "explanation." then, describe how you can make more progress in the same field as "more progress." schedule a set a date for each task to be finished so that you get it completed.

Have them on your table or list of functions. Can you see how much momentum this exercise will give you in your life?

If you're a boss, consider making all your workers do this 30-day exercise with you. It's going to keep them focused and develop their confidence. It also fits well as an exercise for the whole family at home. After just 30 days of doing this workout, I've seen a lot of teenager's bloom.

• Build Your Perfect Day

Another essential tool to keep you focused on making your life exactly as you want it to be is to take a few minutes to prepare your next day's schedule and imagine the whole day going exactly as you want it to be. Visualize everybody who's there when you call them, every meeting that begins and finishes on time, all of your goals being dealt with, all of your errands being done with ease, making every sale, and so on. See yourself performing at your best in any situation you experience the next day. This will provide your subconscious all night to focus on finding ways to make it happen just as you've visualized it.

Now get into the habit of visualizing the dream the night before the next day. It's going to make a big difference in your life.

2.3 Clean Up Your Messes and Incompletes

If a cluttered desk is a symbol of a cluttered mind, what does a clean office mean?

See the diagram above. It's called the completion process. Each of these steps — decide, prepare, start, continue, finish, and complete — is needed to accomplish something, get the desired result, and finish. How many of us never complete? We get to the final stage — but leave one last thing unfinished.

Are there places of your life where you went unfinished tasks or failed to close people? Without completing the past, you can't be able to accept the present altogether.

• Failure to Complete Robs You of Valuable Attention Units

Once you launch a project or come to an understanding or consider an improvement that you need to make, it falls into your current memory bank and fills up what I call the focus machine. We can only pay attention to too many items at once, and each promise, resolution, or article on your to-do list leaves fewer concentration units to complete current activities and bring new possibilities and satisfaction into your life.

So why don't people finish? Still, missing places of our life where we are not clear — or where we have emotional and psychological barriers.

• The Four D's of Completion

One way to take care of to-do things is something we've always seen in time management courses: do it, assign it, postpone, or dump it. When you make a piece of paper, then and there you plan to do something about it. If not, drop. If you can do it within 10 minutes, do it immediately. If you want to take care of it yourself, but know it will take longer, delay it by putting it in a folder of the later stuff. If you can't or don't want to take the time, assign it to someone you trust to do the job. Be sure to make the individual report back when the job is done so you know it's complete.

• Creating Space for Something New

Besides technical incompletes, most households often groan under the weight of too much clutter, too many documents, worn-out clothing, unused toys, forgotten personal belongings, and obsolete, damaged, and unneeded objects. In the U.S., the whole ministry industry arose to help homeowners and small businesses store what they can't fit in their homes and offices.

• But Do We Need All This Stuff? Naturally Not.

When you want something different in your life, you will make room for it. That's mentally and physically. If you want a new guy in your life, you will let go of the last one you started dating five years ago. And if you don't, the unspoken message that a new man meets you is "this woman attached to someone else. If we don't throw away clutter and things we don't need anymore, it's because we don't trust our ability to manifest the requisite abundance in our lives to buy new ones. But incomplete like this prevents the wealth from appearing. We need to complete the past to reveal our present more fully.

2.4 Complete the Past with Welcoming the Future

None of us can change our history. However, we can improve our future.

Colin Powell

Sound familiar? Some people go through life with a large anchor behind them, pulling them down. If they could unlock it, they could travel faster and succeed easier. Maybe that's you — keeping past hurts, past unfinished, recent rage, or fear. However, removing these anchors may also be the final step to complete the history and welcome the future.

To embrace the future, we need to let go of the past. One approach is called the absolute truth cycle.

• The Whole Truth Process and Total Truth Letter

The entire truth process, and complete truth letter are tools that help you release past negative feelings and return to your current natural state of love and happiness.

The reason I call it the absolute truth is that we always struggle to express all our true feelings to the person we're upset with. We remain at frustration or pain level and never push beyond it to emotional completion. As a consequence, after such an angry or painful argument, feeling close to — or even relaxed with — the other person can be difficult.

The entire truth cycle helps us communicate our true feelings so we can restore our normal state of love, closeness, and cooperation.

The period is not intended to encourage us to dump or discharge negative emotions onto another, but to help us to pass beyond the negative emotions and release them so that we can return to the state of love and acceptance that is our normal state of being and from which happiness and creativity will flourish.

• Forgive and Move On

As long as you don't forgive anyone in your mind that will occupy rent-free space.

Isabelle Holland

Though discussing forgiveness in a book about how to be more active can seem odd, the reality is that rage, frustration, and desire for vengeance will waste precious resources that could be diverted into constructive, goal-oriented action.

Under the law of attraction, we have already addressed that you draw more of whatever emotions you encounter. Feeling pessimistic, bitter, and unforgiving about a past hurt just makes sure you attract more in your life.

• Forgive and Return to The Present

In the business world, in families, and in personal relationships, we too need to come from the palace of love and forgiveness — to let go so we can move on. Forgive a business associate who lied to you and hurt you financially. You need to forgive a coworker who took credit for your job or gossiped behind your back. You must forgive an ex-spouse who cheated you, then got nasty during a divorce. You don't have to accept or trust them again. But you must learn the lessons, forgive, and move on.

Forgiving puts you back in the present — where good things can happen to you and where you can act to build potential opportunities for yourself, your team, your company, and your family. Staying mired in the past consumes precious resources and robs you of the leverage you need to create what you want.

Whatever makes you like. You also know that harboring bitterness, holding a grudge, and constantly resuming the same hate will harm you even more. Forgive just means giving it up for yourself — not for them.

2.5 Face What Is Not Functioning

Evidence fails to exist if they are overlooked.

Aldous Huxley

If you're going to be more active, you must get out of denial and face what doesn't work in your life.

Defend or deny how violent and dangerous the workplace is? Excuses for your miserable marriage? Do you deny your energy deficit, extra weight, ill health, or physical fitness? Do you fail to notice a steady downward trend over the last three months? Are you holding off confronting an employee not performing at an appropriate performance standard? Good people face these situations squarely, listen to the warning signs, and take effective action, no matter how unpleasant or demanding.

• Note the Yellow Warnings

Yellow warnings are just the little signals you get that something's wrong. Your teen returns from school late. Strange notes in client mail. A buddy or neighbour's unusual remark. Often, we choose to notice these warnings and respond, but more often than not, we simply want to ignore them. We prefer not to know that anything is a mistake. Generally, facing what doesn't work in your life means you'll have to do something unpleasant. It means you can need to practice more self-discipline, challenge others, risk not being accepted, ask what you want, demand respect instead of settling for an abusive relationship, or maybe even quit your work. Yet if you don't want to do such awkward stuff, you'll also justify tolerating a situation that doesn't work. What's denial look like?

Although our life's unfortunate circumstances can be embarrassing, humiliating, and painful, we sometimes live with them or — worse — hide them behind myths, commonly held beliefs, and platitudes.

Occasionally, we'll also make up excuses why anything that doesn't work is working, not knowing that if we only understood the bad situation earlier, fixing it will always be less stressful. It would be simpler, the conditions could be healthier, the issues would be easier to solve, we could be more open to those concerned, we would feel better about ourselves, and we would have more credibility. Yet we must resolve our skepticism.

On the other hand, productive people are more committed to figuring out why things go wrong and fixing them than protecting their position or preserving their ignorance.

In the company, they look in real numbers at the hard facts, rather than recalculating the figures to look useful to stockholders. They're fair and practical. We can look at what is, and not hide it, and refute it.

Adding more of what doesn't work won't change it

Charles j. Givens

• Know When to Keep Them, Know When to Fold Them

 A large part of getting out of denial is being good at identifying unpleasant circumstances and then trying to do something about them. It still amazes me how difficult to understand and determine for most people — even when it comes to alcoholism and opioid abuse. For many addicts, their relationships fail, their businesses collapse, they lose their home and also end up on skid row until they know that they don't work for them.

Luckily, most of our issues are less severe than drugs, but this doesn't promote understanding or decision. Take your work, for example. Are you avoiding what you'd like to do? Worse still, do you always note how happy and fulfilled you are when not? Are you living a lie?

Workaholics are a prime example of such denial. A high-pressure lifestyle does not work long-term for anyone. Still, most workaholics will defend it with statements like "I'm making great money," "this is how I support my family," "it's how I get ahead," and "I have to do it to succeed in the workplace." as we've already discussed, defending and justifying a bad situation is just a type of denial.

• Denial Is Based on the Premise

That anything much worse will happen if we stop denying and taking action. In other words, we hate meeting facts squarely.

Many therapists will inform you that, given apparent signs that their spouse is having an affair, many people do not question their spouse. We don't want the possibility that the marriage might be over. But you must face what doesn't work first.

The good news is, the more comfortable you are handling awkward circumstances. When you meet one thing that doesn't work, the next time you have the slightest inkling, you're more likely to take decisive action.

2.6 Embrace Change

Accept transition is life's practice. So those who just look past or present will miss the future.

John f. Kennedy's

Unavoidable. For starters, your body and cells change right now. Changing terrestrial. Economy, technology, how we do business, and how we interact change.

And while you can resist the transition and probably be swept away by it, you can also choose to comply, adapt, and profit from it.

• Where Should You Grow?

When change occurs, you can either work with it or learn how to profit from it, or you can fight it and ultimately get overwhelmed. That's your decision.

When you embrace change as an unavoidable part of life, finding ways to use new moves to make your life more productive, simpler, and more satisfying, and your life will work much better.

You'll view transition as growth potential and unique experiences. Things could turn out, maybe even for the better, if only you embrace this transition as an opportunity to develop something new and better.

• How to Embrace Change

Realize that there are two kinds of development — cyclical transformation and systemic change — none of which you can monitor.

Cyclical transition, like the stock market transition, occurs many times a year. Prices go up and down. Bull markets and corrections exist. We see seasonal weather changes, American public holiday spending, more summer travel, etc. Changes are occurring in cycles, and, honestly, most of them we embrace as a natural part of life.

But there are also systemic changes — like when the machine was invented and how we live, work, get our news, and make purchases. Structural reforms are the types of changes that don't go back to doing stuff as before. And these are the kinds of improvements you can sweep away if you resist.

Remember when you felt a transition, but resisted. Maybe it's a transition, a working switch, a change in suppliers, a change in your company's technology, a change in management, or even your teenager going to college — a shift you'd have to deal with because you think it's the worst thing in the world.

What happened after you surrendered? Eventually, your life improved?

Could you look back and think, "Wow, I'm glad that happened? Look at the finally got me beautiful.

2.7 Turn Your Inner Critic into an Inner Coach

A man is literally what he thinks.

Research shows that the average person — that means you! — talks about 50,000 times a day to himself or herself. And most of that self-talk is about yourself, and according to psychoanalysts, it's 80 percent negative — things we know from the research that these thoughts have a powerful effect on us. They affect our behaviour, our physiology, and our motivation to act. Our negative thoughts are controlling our behaviour. They make us stumble, they spill things, they forget our lines, they break out in a sweat, they breathe shallowly, they feel scared — and taken to the extreme, they can even paralyze or kill us.

• Your Negative Thoughts Affect Your Body

We also know from polygraph tests that your body reacts to your thoughts — change your temperature, heart rate, blood pressure, breathing rate, muscle tension, and how much your hands sweat. When you're hooked up with a lie detector, you're asked a question like, "did you take the money?" your hands are going to get colder, your heart is going to beat faster, your blood pressure is going to rise, your breathing is going to get faster, your muscles are going to get tighter, and your hands will sweat if you take the money and you lie about it. These kinds of physiological changes occur not only when you lie, but also when you react to every thought you think. Every cell in your body is affected by every thought you've got.

Negative thoughts harm your body — weakening you, making you sweat, and making you upright. Positive thoughts positively affect your body, making you more relaxed, focused, and alert. Positive thoughts will cause the brain to secrete endorphins, reduce pain, and increase pleasure.

• Talk to Yourself Like a Winner

So, what if you could learn to talk to yourself like a winner instead of a loser? What if you could turn your negative self-talk into positive self-talk? What if you could silence your thoughts of lack and limitation and replace them with thoughts of unlimited possibilities? What if you could replace the language of the victim in your thoughts with the language of empowerment? And what if you could turn your inner critic, who judges your every move, into a supportive inner coach who would encourage you and give you confidence when you face new situations and risks? Well, that's all possible with a little awareness, focus, and intent.

• Stomp Those ANTs

Psychiatrist Daniel g. Amen has named the limiting thoughts that we hear in our head, ANTs — automatic negative thoughts. The same as real ants at a picnic, your ants can ruin your life experience. Daemen recommends that you learn to suppress the ants.

You have to be aware of the first, and then you have to shake them off and stomp them by challenging them. Finally, you need to replace them with more positive and assertive thoughts.

The key to dealing with any sort of negative thinking is to realize that you are ultimately in charge of whether to listen to or agree to any thinking. Just because you don't think it — or hear it — is true.

You've got to be mindful of the first person to speak back to your ants. Write down every negative thought you think or say aloud, and every negative thought you hear someone else say — for three whole days! (Make sure that two days are working days, and that 1 is a weekend day.) This is the best way to raise your awareness of your ants. Here are a few more.

Ask your spouse or wife, babies, roommates, and colleagues to catch you and make a dollar fine any time they hear you say something negative.

• Different Types of Ants

It's helpful to understand some of the different types of ants that might attack you. When you recognize these kinds of ants, you realize they are irrational thoughts that need to be challenged and replaced. Here are some of the most common types of ants and how to stomp them.

• Learn How to Play the Appreciation Game

In every situation, look for things to appreciate. You become more appreciative and hopeful as you consciously search for the best, which is a prerequisite for building the life of your dreams. Well, just look for the good.

A powerful exercise to build your appreciation muscle is to take 7 minutes every morning to write down all the things you value in your life. This is recommended as a daily ritual for the rest of your life; however, if you think it is excessive, do it for at least 30 to 40 days. It's going to create a huge change in how you see the world.

• Catastrophic Predicting

In a catastrophic prediction, you create the worst possible scenario in your mind and then act as if it were a certainty. This might include predicting that your sales prospect won't be interested in your product, that the person you're attracted to will reject your request to go out on a date, that your boss won't give you a raise, or that the plane you're flying on will crash. Replace "she's probably going to laugh at me if I ask her for a date" with "I don't know what she's going to do. She might say yes.

• Guilt-Tripping

Guilt happens when you think words like they should, must, must, or must. Here are some examples: I should spend more time studying at my bar exam. I've got to exercise more. As soon as we feel we need to do something, we create an internal resistance to doing it.

You're going to be more effective if you replace guilt-tripping with phrases like I want to, it supports my goals to, it would be smart to, it's in my best interest to, Guilt is never productive. It's going to stand in the way of achieving your goals. So, let the emotional barrier to success go.

• How to Silence Your Performance Critic?

Have you ever taught a lesson, given a speech, made a sales presentation, participated in an athletic event, performed in a performance, performed a concert, or performed any kind of work, and then found yourself on the way home listening to that voice in your head telling you how you messed up, what you should have done differently, how you could have done it better? I'm sure you've. And if you listen to that voice for a long time, it can weaken your self-confidence, lower your self-esteem, and even demoralize and eventually paralyze you. Here's another easy but effective way to shift contact from judgment and criticism to clarification and help.

Note again that your inner critic's deepest underlying motive is to help you be better at what you do, tell your inner critic to stop criticizing and berating you, or stop listening. Tell your inner voice you're not ready to hear any more character assassinations, name-calling, or browsing — only concrete steps you can take to do things better next time. It removes put-downs and focuses on "improvement incentives" for the next event. Now the inner critic is an inner mentor, pointing out ways to boost potential performance. There's nothing you can do to change the past. You can only learn and improve your performance next time.

When you turn the topic to a non-emotional discussion of opportunities for progress, attitude switches from negative to positive.

Here's a helpful tip. Since memory research tells us that a new idea only lasts about 40 seconds in short-term memory, and then it's gone, it's essential to write down these ideas and place them in a file you'll check before your next output. Otherwise, you can lose useful feedback.

2.8 Transcend the Restricting Convictions

You don't disagree with your subconscious mind. It acknowledges the decrees of the conscious mind.

Many of us believe that our achievements are minimal — whether they believe in our abilities, whether they believe in what it takes to succeed, whether they believe in what we can relate to other people, and even traditional beliefs that modern science or studies have long debunked. Beyond your restricted expectations is a crucial first step to success. You will learn how to recognize beliefs that hinder you and replace them with positive feelings that help your success.

• You Are Capable and Worthy of Love

Many people do not believe that you are capable and deserving of the love of the struggles of life or that it is worthy of love — the two critical pillars of high self-esteem. Believing you can do anything in your life means you don't have any more fear of anything. And think about it — didn't you manage anything you've ever experienced? Stuff that was even tougher than you thought was? A loved one's death, divorce, broken? Loss of a friend, work, money, credibility, youth? Such tasks were complicated, but you did. So, you can do whatever happens to you too. If you have that, your confidence will grow.

Believing you worthy of love means that, with reverence and integrity, you think I deserve to be appropriately handled. I deserve somebody's love and adoration. I expect a close and satisfying relationship. I'm not going to accept something less than I deserve. I'm going to do something to build that for myself.

2.9 Build Four New Patterns of Performance a Year

Psychologists advise us that up to 90% of our behavior is normative. 90 percent! There are hundreds of activities you do the same every day, from the moment you wake up in the morning until the moment when you retire in the evening. This includes the way you shower, dress, eat breakfast, read the newspaper, brush your teeth, drive to work, arrange your office, shop at the store, and clean your home. Over the years, you have established a collection of deeply ingrained behaviors that dictate how well every aspect of your life functions, from your job and your income to your health and your relationships.

The good news is that routines help free up your mind when your body is on automatic. It helps you to schedule your day while you are in the shower and chat with your fellow passengers while you are driving your car. The bad news is that you will get locked into unconscious self-defeating behavior patterns that hinder your development and restrict your performance. Your habits produce your current level of results. More than likely, if you want to achieve higher rates of productivity, you are going to need to change some of your habits (not returning phone calls, staying up too late watching television, making derogatory remarks, eating fast food every day, smoking, being late for appointments, spending more than you earn) and replacing them with more successful habits (returning phone calls within 24 hours, having 8 hours of sleep each day, reading for an hour a day, exercising four days a week, eating nutritious food, being on time, and saving 10 percent of your income).

• Good or Poor, Habits Always Yield Results Performance

Is a matter of knowing and consistently following transparent, simple practices that always lead to success?

Robert j. Ringer

The patterns decide the outcomes. Good people don't just rise to the top. Getting there needs concerted action, personal discipline, and plenty of effort every day to make things happen. The behaviors you build from this day forward will eventually decide how your future unfolds.

One of the challenges with people with poor habits is that the consequences of their bad habits typically don't turn up until much later in life. When you form a persistent bad habit, life will finally give you results. You may not like the effects, but the experience will always deliver them. The truth is, if you keep on doing things a certain way, you will still get a predictable result. Bad attitudes cause adverse effects. Positive habits create positive consequences.

• What Will You Do If You Took on Four New Patterns A Year?

If you use these techniques to build only four new habits a year, five years from now, you'll have 20 new success habits that will get you all the money you want, the excellent loving relationships you want, a happier, more energized body, plus all kinds of new opportunities.

Start by listing four new habits you would like to develop in the next year. Work on one new pattern per fifth. If you focus consistently on developing one new habit every 13 weeks, you won't burden yourself with an endless list of new year's resolutions…and evidence now shows that if you practice activity for 13 weeks—whether it is meditating for 20 minutes a day, flossing your teeth, updating your goals, or writing thank-you notes to your clients—it will be yours for life. By gradually adding one action at a time, you will significantly change your overall lifestyle.

Perhaps the most effective way to remain on track is to follow the "no exceptions rule."

3

Attitudes to Risk in Business

Risk attitude is at a high level and demonstrates the inherent tendency or fundamental existence of stakeholders or organizations, whether or not they are willing to take risks. It is a response chosen by stakeholders that are informed by their understanding of a particular situation.

There are three significant types of risk attitudes.

Risk Seeker:

People who are at risk. They don't overthink about the consequences if the danger materializes. They're more focused on the benefits they're going to get.

Risk-Averse:

 Risk-averse people do not like uncertainty. We plan to take the most likely course, even if it is the least rewarding.

Risk Neutral:

Risk-neutral people are very analytical and consider both pros and cons before they determine whether or not to take risks.

Danger attitude is difficult to quantify, but that doesn't mean we can't do anything about it. That would be very risky, in reality. The project manager must consider the attitudes of the stakeholders to formulate an acceptable risk response.

Risk attitude is very similar to risk appetite. Risk appetite is the ability or desire of individuals or organizations to take risks to achieve a particular goal. All are high-level and difficult to describe. They affect and complement one another.

3.1 Approaches for Assessing Risk Attitudes

Three common strategies in the research literature are considered:

1. The selection list (sometimes referred to as the multiple price list) methods (e.g., Cheetal. 1987, Tversky and Kahneman 1992, holt and Laurie 2002) provides a table of binary choices structured so that, as the respondent moves through the table, it can be expected to turn from one side to the other at some point. When decisions are made between risky alternatives, the switching point is believed to be representative of the risk attitude of the person.

2. The rating method (e.g., Binswanger 1980 and 1981, Eckel and Grossman 2002) provides a set of options and asks the respondent to decide which choice is the most suitable. When applied to a collection of risky prospects with various combinations of spread and return, the aim is to define the risk attitude of the person as expressed in its most favored equilibrium between mean and variance. We also expanded this process to achieve a complete rating over the entire range of options.

3. The allocation process (e.g., Looms 1991) provides the respondent with a budget and allows it to be allocated between various state-related statements. When applied to risk, the chosen allocation – in conjunction with information on the rate of exchange between claims – will allow the risk attitude of the person to be inferred.

3.2 Risk Attitudes of Sustainable Entrepreneurs vs. Traditional Entrepreneurs

Entrepreneurs who start a company to meet both self-interest and mutual interests by addressing unmet social and environmental needs are generally referred to as viable entrepreneurs. Compared to traditional entrepreneurs, we argue that sustainable entrepreneurs face unique challenges when setting up their companies because of the disparity between the development and redistribution of private property and social capital. It is believed that sustainable entrepreneurs (1) feel more hindered by perceived obstacles, such as the institutional climate, when starting a company, and (2) have a different risk attitude and perception than typical entrepreneurs. We use two waves on entrepreneurship, which provides information on startup motives, startup obstacles, and risk perceptions of approximately 3000 (prospective) business owners across 33 countries. We consider that sustainable entrepreneurs also experience more institutional barriers in terms of a lack of political, administrative, and informational support at a business startup than typical entrepreneurs. Furthermore, there are no significant variations in perceptions of risk or perceived financial risks between sustainable and everyday entrepreneurs. Sustainable entrepreneurs, however, are more likely to fear personal failure than conventional entrepreneurs, clarified by their diverse, complex stakeholder relations. These insights can serve as an essential signal for both governments and private capital providers in enhancing the institutional environment.

3.3 Effect of Risk Attitudes in the Startup Process

• The Impact of Risk Attitudes on Entrepreneurial Survival

Risk attitudes have an impact on not only the decision to become an entrepreneur but also to the success and failure rates of entrepreneurs. Whereas recent work underpins the theoretical proposition of a secure link between risk perceptions and the decision to become an entrepreneur, the effects on survival are not as straightforward. Psychological work posits an inverse u-shaped relationship between risk attitudes and entrepreneurial survival. Based on recent waves of the German socio-economic panel (step), we analyze the degree to which risk attitudes affect survival rates of entrepreneurs. The empirical findings suggest that persons whose risk attitudes are in the medium range live substantially longer as entrepreneurs than do persons with extremely low or high risks.

• Effects of Risk Attitude and Controllability Assumption on Risk Ratings

Risk evaluation based on probability-impact (p-I) scores is the most commonly used method in project-oriented industries such as the building industry.

However, there are numerous concerns regarding the use of the p-I rating methodology as there are variables and assumptions that are concealed within the risk ratings that cannot be communicated to decision-makers for a credible risk assessment. This study aimed at exploring biases, primarily how risk attitude and perceptions on risk controllability (the knowledge of control bias) influencing subjective risk ratings assigned by experts during risk assessment of international construction projects. Results showed that as perceived controllability increased, expert risk ratings tended to be lower. There was a mild association between risk attitude and risk scores. Risk attitude and expectations on controllability were also moderately related, and their combined effect on risk ratings varied according to different risk scenarios. Risk ratings were influenced by the risk attitudes of experts, mainly when the country risk level was high. At the same time, assumptions on controllability tended to affect risk ratings more significantly when the country risk level was low. While the questionnaire results about the effect of biases on risk ratings are relevant only within the context of this research, results may have some general implications for developing new methods that can illustrate and monitor the secret factors in subjective risk ratings. Assumption-based thinking and information elicitation on risk ratings, together with underlying assumptions by group decision making, can decrease the impact of the illusion of control bias during the risk assessment process.

• Domain Effects and Financial Risk Attitudes

We examined whether financial risk expectations are based on the economic environment (i.e., the context) in which the risky choice choices are presented. Previous studies have shown that risk perceptions change when gamblers are given as profits, losses, or as insurance.

Our research addresses this explicitly by providing choices between similar gambles, framed in terms of seven financial realms. Three factors were identified, explaining 68.6 percent of the variance: factor 1 (positive)-opportunity to win, pension allocation, and work wage change; factor 2 (positive-complex)-investments and mortgage buying; factor 3 (negative)-possibility of loss and insurance. The inspection of the approach showed background impact on risk perceptions across the seven scenarios. We also found that the widely held belief that women are more risk-averse cannot be verified with the background structure suggested in this research; however, it is agreed that in the students' population, the variation between genders may be considerably less. These findings indicate that our financial risk attitude tests could be tapping into a robust dimension of "context dependency" of importance to real-world decision making.

3.4 Entrepreneurial Development and Success

Is a risky but required process for startups to thrive? Growth may be measured for staff, clients, sales, profitability, income, geographic locations, and other dimensions. Whatever form of development, hurdles always exist. An entrepreneur who knows and deliberately takes risks will have a chance to grow, while no one who is reluctant to take risks will.

It defines growth-related risks and benefits. This then explores six challenges facing entrepreneurs when trying to grow a business: company culture, networks, strategic planning, capital, company structure, and skill growth.

• Company Culture and Networks

The personalities of a startup's founders can be a significant driving force in the startup's growth. The founders must decide the company's reach and vision, as well as the company's risks and deals. Founders are responsible for defining business culture. As the business expands, entrepreneurs must communicate nationally and internationally with vendors, rivals, consumers, and investors. Founders with national and foreign connections are more likely to expand their businesses than those with regional connections. A broad network helps businesses to easily grow and find partners in new areas, enabling them to broaden their customer base rapidly. Being able to select from different markets and being able to evolve internally allows a business a greater opportunity to respond to an evolving global marketplace. This, in effect, enables steady growth.

• Strategic Planning

Companies need short- and long-term strategic planning to succeed. Long-term performance includes good day-to-day management and strategic decisions. It also requires that these are not at long-term program costs. Companies with fewer short- and long-term preparation are at higher risk of failure. Many firms seek short-term contracts and fast profits without considering their choices' long-term effects.

It's rare for a firm to be frustrated when a long-term approach doesn't produce immediate results. Many companies don't understand that setting a long-term target and making strategic decisions for that target won't produce immediate positive results. It may be difficult to implement short-term strategies when aligning with long-term objectives. Still, it is important to offer the firm a vision that allows employee concentration and cohesion.

A business that only chases short-term returns will make a profit for a while but will have a difficult time continuing to expand. Achieving regular achievements and directing behaviors towards a long-term target can be an efficient way to handle short-term tasks. This allows short-term targets to be set in the light of the broader picture, thus allowing each instance to be tailored for different circumstances. It's a good idea for an organization and its workers to know their 1, 2, 3, and 5-year plans to unify priorities and allow accountability on how the business meets its milestones.

• Money Matters

Many businesses plan incorrectly or take too many chances and face fiscal issues. Lack of capital is a startup bug. Over-optimism on the cash available may be a startup's deadly feature. Because of high startup failure rates, it's hard to attract significant sums of funding if you can't guarantee a return on investment. Most banks refuse to finance startups. It is also difficult to receive venture capital and angel financing, as there are far more businesses seeking these funds than funds are available. For others, government services that are typically less established, and therefore have less competition, provide an alternative source of funding. Export credit to suppliers is also possible.

Many startups bootstrap as a way to get started, because this approach won't incur big debt. The best source of startup funding is consumer purchasing goods and services. This method makes growth with stable income growth. Fiscal problems are common and recurrent in a startup lifecycle. Being aware that such challenges would arise and being prepared with a strategy for a limited budget helps a company to expand with far less risk than one that thought the funding would be there when needed. Financial planning will be an important part of short- and long-term business plans, with budgets rarely having as much money as an organization needs or expects.

• Company Structure

Business structure when an organization is small, all information sources may be concentrated into one person, usually the founder, allowing that person to make decisions quickly based on information from the source.

During and after growth, as the organization loses some internal control, it is often not possible for a single person to monitor all the information without structured communication channels.

As the business expands, handling everyday activities becomes increasingly complicated if the same organizational framework is retained. This creates a double impact, giving the central figure less time to communicate with others as they spend increasing time allocations trying to manage operations. Many companies find this challenging in the first growth cycle as the founder is always uncomfortable with giving up total control of all facets of the business. With a deep in-house framework of common rules and values, these changes will flow smoothly. This encourages workers to work towards a target rather than a particular task. Even though tumultuous development, the goal remains the same, letting employees know what is anticipated and what to do.

• Skills Development

Inter-company training is a good way to achieve stable growth. Employee preparation will concentrate on the company's needs, rather than what's beyond the company. Through a holistic training strategy, a deep framework can be developed that allows workers to concentrate and work towards goals. Training promotes growth changes when workers know what is expected of them in the company's broader context, enabling them to continue to work efficiently even as the individual aspects of their employment shift. Training instills a sense of career in people expecting to continue and develop with the business. Training helps the mindsets of workers to be adapted to that of the business community, making them ideally suited to the business.

3.5 Exiting Entrepreneurship

It is also helpful to start preparing for an exit in the early stages of the company's life. If the goal is to have an IPO, to get acquired by Google quickly or to pass on the family business to children, early planning will help founders organize their company towards their desired outcome.

Your exit strategy will affect many aspects of your company, such as its legal structure, the types of revenue models you should follow, the tradeoffs between investing for long vs. Short-term growth, the types of investors you should try, etc. Even if you leave the business because of burnout, business failure, or boredom with your work, it still pays to prepare in advance for the exit. By reasoning about different exit strategies from the outset, entrepreneurs will optimize their take-home return on their investment and sweat equity.

- It Is Essential to Prepare the Exit Strategy as Early as Possible

Even if they are not intended to leave your company shortly, it is necessary to think about your options and have a plan in place. There are two main explanations for this. First, a clear exit strategy helps potential investors to make reasonable estimates of the timetable and expected rate of return on their investment, raising the likelihood of investment by an angel or VC. Secondly, choosing how you want to exit allows you to arrange business such that it optimizes your return in case of such an exit.

Many equity investments by angel investors and VCS are dependent on the successful business exit to see a return on their investment. This ensures that entrepreneurs are highly unlikely to receive equity capital from potential investors unless they include an exit strategy in their pitch and business plan. Entrepreneurs will work and know by what means and how quickly similar businesses in similar markets have been able to exit. In the case of externally-funded startups, most frequently, this would be by the acquisition by a larger company and sometimes by an IPO. Additionally, company owners should give investors an idea of the size of their future returns.

If your exit plans include stepping back from day-to-day activities and transforming your company into a cash cow, you'll want to look for a business model where the business is not dependent on you. This would allow you to create a model that is systematized such that it works the same way every time, and can be managed by ordinary people without needing super-stars like you. You will be focused on your business rather than in your business so that the company can stand on its own.

• IPO Ready

If you have been able to rapidly grow your business to a point where there is broad acceptance of its success, you may be prepared to accept public investors for your company via an IPO. Usually, you need a comprehensive and diversified consumer or client base, a stellar team, increasing sales, and competitive financials to achieve this stage. However, the last criterion is often overlooked in high-growth industries such as technology.

In us, you would usually need $10 million in pre-tax earnings over the last three years, at least $2 million of which would have been raised in each of the previous two years. For a more detailed overview of the financial criteria of an IPO, read this. The stock exchanges often offer alternative approaches based on metrics such as market cap and sales for large businesses that do not meet the income conditions.

Since an IPO requires significant effort and expense, you can only consider it when you have reached a scale that can justify such costs. An effective IPO can provide a perfect exit strategy for the entrepreneur who wants to end his involvement with the company.

• Market Volatility

Sometimes, owners of successful companies plan to cash out because of volatility about potential market developments.

If you are selling in the luxury market, in times of financial crisis, your target customer may have the less disposable income to spend on your goods. Often, changes in business regulations or government policy may adversely affect a company. In another scenario, a rival enters the market and challenges your business model. Following umber's disruption of the taxi market, especially in the USA, many owners of traditional taxi businesses have looked for a way to exit.

In each of these cases, it can make sense for the entrepreneur to pre-emptively prepare and exit the company.

• Company Failure

If you start losing money after having tried several solutions to stabilize the company, it may be better to call it quits. Quitting may be a smart move if you are many years into your venture and still have no traction; customers even respond to your sales pitch with a blank look.

You can read some interesting stories about failed companies here. Continued operations can result in additional losses, which will further erode your net worth.

• Exhaustion

Many people in business struggle with financial volatility, transactions falling through with investors or clients, and continuously evolving business models. The more creative the business concept, the less likely the average person is going to respond to you; feelings of depression are not unusual. Some problems take a long-term toll on mental health.

Research by Dr. Michael Freeman, clinical professor of psychiatry at the University of California and an entrepreneur, found that 49 percent of entrepreneurs have mental health issues. The most popular of these is depression (30 percent), while 27 percent have anxiety. Stress is a significant contributory factor to both of these conditions, and some businessmen chose to leave their businesses to avoid burning out entirely.

• Lifestyle Change

Perhaps your company doesn't suit your present lifestyle anymore. There may be many reasons: you could have achieved a sure financial success and want to spend the rest of your life. You may have started a family and want to spend time with them instead of working 60-hour weeks. You may have developed a new interest, or rediscovered an old one.

Finally, when you start physically slowing down, it's understandable you'd want to sell your company and focus your money on your family rather than working all the time.

• Business Exit Strategies

Ultimately, the following five techniques are available for an entrepreneur to exit a company.

IPO

When businesses first release their shares to the public through a stock exchange listing, this is known as an initial public offering or short IPO. It is an exit in the sense that institutional investors (such as VC and Pe investors) are likely to see a return on investment through enhanced equity values, rather than in the feeling that the founders would end their engagement with the company. But after an IPO, the entrepreneur can sell his equity to the public and can thus exit the company. Is used to be the accessible exit mode, but IPO rates have decreased after the internet bubble burst in 2000.

Although IPOs are relatively uncommon relative to the number of startups generated each year, the reputation and financial compensation benefits of accessing public capital can be overwhelming. Companies going public usually get a lot of media attention; founding stock may be worth 8 or 9 figures. Indeed, being a billionaire is hard unless you own a public company.

Sadly, IPOs are only feasible if a large-scale business succeeds. IPOs are also expensive; average over $1,000,000. Investment bankers may charge large sums for underwriting fees and other costs associated with compliance with accounting and reporting regulations.

• Merger or Acquisition

An excellent exit choice is to combine or buy another company.

Complementary company mergers add economies of scale to the newly-formed sector. Find a capitalized acquirer who can close deals efficiently and professionally. In an acquisition, the acquirer will take over the entrepreneur's equity, offering him an exit.

You should be careful to run the business to be bought by one client. If your intended acquirer isn't interested, you risk developing a product so specialized that you won't buy any other company.

• Sale to A Friendly Buyer

Instead of selling to an unknown rival often passing the company to relatives, family, staff, or managers you know well makes more sense. Such a beautiful sale is also a successful exit strategy.

Selling to someone you know and trust, the extra familiarity, and confidence translates into less due diligence on both sides, minimizing legal costs for those involved. When you sell to managers involved in the sector, the transition challenges are minimal.

On the other hand, leaving the company to multiple children without adequate preparation will precipitate messy legal battles for control that can divide families from chaos. If you sell to a relative, and later conflicts occur, you risk destroying a friendship. Alternatively, if you sell to agents who are also your mates, it's possible to concentrate so much on your bond that you don't demand as high a sale price as you would otherwise have.

• Retire Without Selling the Company

Often it may be possible to retire without selling the company without selling it outright. In this situation, you remain a shareholder, allowing you to profit from its dividends without active day-to-day operations.

The essential advantage of this strategy is to keep collecting daily payments for little to no work. When you retire, this can be an outstanding lifestyle supplement. If you're younger and still have business goals, you can use these funds to start a new company.

For succeeding in this exit plan, you need a reliable team and streamlined structures and processes to keep the company running without regular involvement.

• Liquidation

Is considered to be liquidated when it ceases, ceases its doors and sells any remaining properties. Any proceeds are split among the shareholders after repayment.

If you're burnt out, itching to start another company immediately or wanting to retire as soon as possible, it has the benefit of being extremely quick. No share deals or lengthy meetings with attorneys. Since settlement is final, there's no need to think about the buyer's trustworthiness. On the other hand, the arrangement is the least financially lucrative exit option because it networks the market value of the company's assets and nothing more. Intangibles like client lists, prestige, and business partnerships can be precious, and you'll probably leave a lot on the table by not taking the time to find a buyer.

3.6 Entrepreneurial Self-Efficacy, Risk Attitudes, and Optimism

Although an entrepreneurial career needs some degree of optimism and confidence, excessive optimism, and overconfidence can harm entrepreneurial success. By analyzing perceptual differences between students and professors, we determine whether university students are excessively positive about the outcomes they anticipate from an entrepreneurial career, as well as overconfident in their perceptions of obstacles to entrepreneurship. Overall, results indicate students are more optimistic, but not more enthusiastic than faculty. Students more confident and fulfilled than their professors often feel more ambitious and have better ambitious goals than their peers.

4

Build a Successful Team

We can do so little alone; we can do so much together.

Helen Keller

4.1 Stay Focused on Your Core Genius

You've got a core genius inside you — something you love to do and do so well that you don't feel like charging people for it. It's effortless and a lot of fun for you. And if you could make money to do that, you'd make it your life's work.

Successful people also believe this. That's why they've put their core genius first. They're focusing on it — and delegating everything else to other people on their team.

Compare that to other people in the world who are going through life doing everything, even those tasks that are a bad actor that could be done cheaper, better, and faster by someone else. They can't find the time to focus on their core genius, because they can't delegate even the smallest tasks.

• Become A Con Artist Doing What You Love to Do

The most significant mistake people make in life is not trying to make a living doing what they enjoy the most.

Malcolm s. Forbes

Strategic coach Dan Sullivan once said that all entrepreneurs are con artists. They're going to get other people to pay them to practice getting better at what they love to do.

• Think about that.

Consider the Chicago cubs' great Sammy Sosa baseball. It takes about 1 second to hit the home run — as long as it takes the ball to hit the bat. He earns $10,625,000 for about 70 seconds of batting time a year, so he's gotten good at making the bat meet the ball. That's where he's going to make his money. That's where he's been putting all his time — practicing and getting ready for the bat to meet the ball. He has found his core genius and devotes most of his waking hours to perfecting his talent.

Of course, most of us aren't on par with tiger woods, tony Robbins, or Sammy Sosa, but the fact is that we could learn a lot from their level of focus.

For example, many salespeople spend more time on account management than they do on phone sales when they can hire a part-time administrator (or share the cost with another salesperson) to do this time-consuming detailed work.

Don't let this be your destiny. Identify your core genius, then delegate completely to free up more time to concentrate on what you love to do.

• Do What You Love — Money Will Follow

Starting to make money is the biggest mistake in life. Do what you feel like you're doing, and if you're good enough, the capital's coming.

4.2 Redefine Time

The world is entering a new time zone, and one of the most challenging adjustments that people have to make is their fundamental concepts and beliefs about time management.

Dan Sullivan

The most successful people I know are producing superior results while still maintaining a balance between work, family, and recreation in their lives. To achieve this, they use a unique planning system that structures their time into three very different types of days that are pre-scheduled to ensure the highest payoff for their efforts, while still allowing abundant amounts of free time to pursue their interests.

Dan Sullivan, president of the strategic coach, has created a great system that I use, called the entrepreneurship time system. It divides all your time into three kinds of days: focus days, buffer days, and free days.

• Start Scheduling

The key to getting more open days and best results days in your life is to sit down and plan. By checking out how many best results days, preparation days, and open days you spend every month right now, you can work to increase the number of best results days and exact 24-hour free days on your calendar and reduce the number of buffer days. With this kind of schedule, you will find yourself creating more results at work, enjoying more fulfillment in your personal life, and experiencing more balance between the two.

4.3 Build A Robust Support Team and Delegate to Them

Every successful person has a powerful group of crucial staff, consultants, vendors, and helpers who do the bulk of their work while free to create new sources of income and new opportunities for success. The world's most significant philanthropists, athletes, entertainers, professionals, and others also have people who manage projects and carry out day-to-day tasks — allowing them to do more for others, hone their craft, practice their sport, and so on.

• The Total Focus Processes

To help you clarify what you should spend your time and what you should be delegating to others, do the following exercise. Your goal is to find the top one, two, or three activities that best use your core genius, bring the most money to you, and create the highest level of enjoyment.

1. Start by listing all the activities that occupy your time, whether they are business-related, personal, or related to your civic organizations or volunteer work. Lists even small tasks, such as returning phone calls, filing, or photocopying.

2. Next, choose from this list that one, two, or three things that you are particularly brilliant at, your individual and unique talents, those things that very few other people can do as well as you can do. Also, choose from this list the three activities that will generate the most income for you or your company. Any action that you're brilliant about, and that makes the most income for you or your company, is the activity where you want to focus the most time and energy.

3. Finally, create a plan to delegate everything else to other people. Charging takes time, training, and patience, but over time, you can keep chipping away at low-payment, non-essential tasks on your list until you do less and less and more of what you're good at. That's how you're creating a brilliant career.

• Seek Out Key "Staff Members"

If you're a business owner — and remember, becoming an entrepreneur early in life is one of the hallmarks of the most successful individuals in modern history — start looking for key staff members now or train your existing staff on the tasks you've identified above. If you're a one-person business, start looking for a dynamic number — two people who can handle your projects, run your programs, book your sales transactions, and take full responsibility for other tasks while you're focusing on what you do best. You can hire them as employees or have them work part-time on a contract basis as your company grows.

• Once You Have Chosen Your Team Members

To trust them, if you don't have an assistant, you're one of them.

Raymond Aaron

If you've chosen carefully, you can start offloading anything and everything that takes you away from focusing on your core genius — even "personal" projects.

Although we often fear that if someone else does work for us, they're not going to be done well — the reality is that there are people who love to do what you hate to do. And they often do a much better job than you would or could do yourself — at a surprisingly low cost.

4.4 Just Say No!

You don't have to be terrorized by other people's expectations of you.

Sue Patton Thiele

Our world is a highly competitive and over-stimulating place, and more and more concentration are needed every day just to stay focused on completing your daily tasks and pursuing your longer-term goals. Because of the explosion in communications technology, we are more accessible to more people than ever before.

• They All Want A Piece of You

Your kids want to ride or borrow a car; your coworkers wish to your input on projects that are not your responsibility, your boss wants you to work overtime to finish the report he needs, your sister wants you to take her kids to the weekend. And an endless stream of telemarketers wants you to subscribe to the local newspaper, contribute to the nearby wildlife sanctuary, or transfer all of your credit card debt to their new card. Even your pets are crying out for more attention.

We suffer under project and productivity overload at work — taking more than we can comfortably do in an unconscious desire to impress others, get ahead, and keep up with other people's expectations. In the meantime, our top priorities have not been addressed.

To accomplish your goals and build your ideal lifestyle, you'll have to do well to say no to all the people and distractions that would otherwise devour you. Reasonable people can say no without feeling guilty.

• If Saying No Is So Important, Why Say It?

Why do we find it so hard to say no to all requests? As kids, many of us learned there's no unacceptable response. Discipline had no reason to respond. Later on, there couldn't have been a justification for poor appraisal or the inability to step up the corporate ladder.

And highly successful people say no all the time — projects, insane deadlines, dubious goals, and disasters of others. We decide to say no as appropriate as saying yes.

Some say no, but I want to refer you to someone else for support. Others also say their schedule, family commitments, deadlines, and even finances are grounds for refusing applications. At the workplace, they consider other approaches to frequent problems of their colleagues, rather than being a victim to someone else's lack of coordination and wrong time management.

"It's not against you; it's for me" one response you may consider helpful in saying no to crisis appeals or people's time-consuming demands is "it's not against you; it's for me." few people can get mad at you for making and standing up for the higher commission. They'll appreciate your consistency and power.

4.5 Hire A Personal Coach

I believe that, unless coached, people will never reach the maximum of their abilities.

Bob Nardelli

You'd never expect an athlete to enter the Olympics without a world-class coach. You wouldn't expect a professional football team to join the stadium without a coaching staff — head coach, offensive coach, defensive coach, and individual team coach. Well, coaching has expanded into the business and personal arena today to include coaches who have been active in your field of interest — and can help you walk the same or even a much larger route.

Some of the best-kept secrets of the wealthy and all the things that successful people do to improve their progress on the road to success are at the top of the list. A coach will help you to articulate your dream and ambitions, guide you through your worries, keep you focused, challenge your ingrained habits and old trends, encourage you to do your best, help you live up to your ideals, teach you how to gain more while working less and keep you focused on your core talent.

Why managing executive coaches aren't just meek. For people who want unambiguous reviews. If coaches share one thing, they are mercilessly results-oriented.

• Gain Clarity

Irrespective of whether the program is designed to achieve a specific business goal — say, increase your real estate listings — or whether it is specifically designed to help you gain more clarity and progress in all aspects of your personal and professional life, a coach can help you:

- Determine your values, vision, mission, purpose, and objectives;

- Determine specific actions;

A personal coach can help you find out what you want to do — and can help you determine the steps and take the action you need to take to get there.

4.6 Mastermind Your Way to Success

When two or more people coordinate in a spirit of harmony and work towards a definite goal or goal, they place themselves in a position, through an alliance, to absorb power directly from the vast store-house of infinite intelligence.

Napoleon hill

We all know that when it comes to solving a problem or creating a result, two heads are better than one. So, imagine having a permanent group of five to six people meeting each week for problem-solving, brainstorming, networking, and encouraging and motivating each other.

This process, called masterminding, is one of the most powerful tools for success in this book. I don't know anyone who has become a super-successful person who has not used the mastermind principle.

• A Process to Accelerate Your Growth

The underlying philosophy of a mastermind group is that more can be achieved in less time when people work together. The mastermind group consists of people who come together regularly — weekly, biweekly, or monthly — to share ideas, thoughts, information, feedback, and resources. By gaining the perspective, knowledge, experience, and support of others in the group, not only can you move beyond your limited view of the world, but you can also advance your personal goals and projects more quickly.

A mastermind community may consist of people from your private industry or career or people from different walks of life. It may focus on business issues, personal issues, or both. But for a mastermind group to be powerfully effective, people must be comfortable enough. Some of the most valuable feedback I've ever received came from members of my mastermind group confronting me with over-committing, selling my services too cheaply, focusing on the trivial, not delegating enough, thinking too small, and playing it safe.

Confidentiality is what allows this level of trust to be built up. Out in the world, we usually manage our personal and corporate image. In a mastermind group, participants can let their hair down, tell the truth about their personal and business life, and feel safe that what is said in the group will remain in the group.

• How to Assemble A Mastermind Group?

Irrespective of its purpose, the key is to choose people who are already where you would like to be in your life — or who are at least one level above you.

If you wish to become a millionaire, and you're only making $60,000 a year now, you'll be better served by gathering together with people who already do more than you do. If you are concerned that people who are already at a higher level than you might not want to be part of a group with you, remember that you are the one who facilitates the meeting. You are organizing, supporting, and building a forum for other people's growth and mastermind needs. A lot of people at a higher level want to get involved simply because they're going to play at a game, they might never take the time to organize for themselves. They'd probably be delighted to mastermind the other people you're going to invite — especially if some of the others are already at their level.

5

Build Positive Relationships

Personal relationships are something which is the fertile soil on which all growth, all accomplishment, all real-life achievement develops.

Ben stein

5.1 Hear Now

Listen a hundred times. Ponder 1,000 times. Chat once.

There's a major difference between hearing — that's only getting communication — and listening, which is the art of paying attention to knowing the full message being transmitted. Unlike only reading someone's story, listening includes eye contact, observing the person's body language, asking for clarity, and listening to the unspoken word.

In the news reporting industry, journalists are educated in the art of active listening — an interview strategy in which reporters listen and understand so well, they can ask better, deeper questions about the information being provided. Active listening is how good news stories develop — and how many of us, too, will strengthen our relationships. Not surprisingly, it also helps ensure accuracy and honesty, two of a journalist's main hallmarks — and two vital qualities in any partnership.

• Be Interested Rather Than Interesting

Another way people fail to listen carefully is to be too worried about being interested in themselves, rather than interested in the person they listen to. They believe the path to success is to continuously talk — show their experience or intellect with words and remarks.

The best way to build relationships and win them over your side is to be genuinely interested in them, listening to learn about them. When the person thinks you're very interested in getting to know them and their feelings, they'll open up far easier and share their true feelings with you.

Act to develop a curiosity attitude. Curious about others, what they feel, how they think, how they see the world. What're their aspirations, dreams, fears? What's their aspiration?

If you want people to collaborate, like you, or open up to you, you must be interested in them. Instead of dwelling on yourself, concentrate on others. Remember what makes them happy.

Your performance increases, and you have more fun. Furthermore, when you're interested, people respond to your interest. They want to be around you. Increase your popularity.

5.2 Have a Heart Talk

Sadly, in so many corporate, educational, and other environments, there is rarely an opportunity for emotions to be shared so that people are not able to focus on the business at hand. There's too much space static mental. It's like trying to bring more water into a full bowl. There's nowhere to go. For the freshwater, you must first pour out the old water.

Emotions are the same. People can't listen until they're heard. They need to get whatever bothers them off their hands. If you're someone who's just come home from college, a parent looking at the report card of your child with all c's, a salesperson trying to sell a new vehicle, or a CEO overseeing the merger between two businesses, you first need to let other people talk about their needs and desires, hopes and aspirations, worries and concerns, hurts and pains, before you think about yours. It opens up a space inside them to listen and take in what you have to say.

• What's A Heart-Talk?

Heart talk is a very organized negotiation mechanism in which eight agreements are strictly adhered to establish protection for a deep contact level to occur without fear of criticism, unsolicited advice, disruption, or hurry. It is a powerful tool used to surface and release any unexpressed emotions that would otherwise interfere with people being completely present to deal with the company. It can be used to build relationships, understanding, and intimacy in home, school, classroom, sports teams, and religious settings.

• How to Use a Heart Talk?

Heart talks are helpful in many situations:

 - Before or after a staff meeting.

 - At the beginning of a business meeting where two separate groups of people come together for the first time.

- During an emotionally stimulating occurrence such as a merger, a huge layoff, a death, a significant athletic defeat, an unwelcome financial failure, or even a tragedy such as terror you'll want to split a group bigger than ten into smaller groups, because if the community is bigger than that, the confidence and protection factors begin to decrease, and that may take too much time.

• How to Conduct a Heart Talk?

The first time you perform a heart chat begins by explaining that you often use a communication system that guarantees a deeper level of listening. A heart talk's framework provides a secure, non-judgmental space that facilitates the constructive − rather than destructive − expression of feelings that, if left unexpressed, can obstruct collaboration, synergy, imagination, and intuition, essential to any venture's efficiency and success.

5.3 Tell the Truth Faster

State the truth faster in question, tell the truth.

Mark twain

Some of us fear, to tell the truth, it's awkward. We fear the consequences − making others unhappy, hurting their feelings, or risking their wrath. Even then, if we don't know the truth and others don't know us the facts, we can't deal with stuff from a foundation.

We've all heard the expression, "the truth will set you free." the reality helps us to be able to live with the way things are, not the way we expect them to be or aspire to be or exploit them with our lies.

Truth always releases our resources. It takes energy to hide the truth, keeps a lie, or act.

• Even If You Tell the Truth?

You feel glad to lose that chest pressure. You feel similar to others. You begin to understand the things you've been avoiding aren't so bad but are generally shared by at least a few in the community. They're not isolated, but part of human society. Yet most remarkably, lifelong migraines vanish. Spastic colons relax and no longer require medication.

Depression lifts and returns alive. People look younger and more vibrant. It's amazing. This teaches us that holding back our truth takes a lot of energy and that energy, when released, can be used to concentrate on achieving greater success in all areas of our lives. We may become less careful and more spontaneous to be our true selves. And as this occurs, knowledge crucial to making things work, and doing things can be exchanged and acted on.

• Why Do You Need Sharing?

For every aspect of our lives, the three issues that most need to be shared are built-up resentments, unmet desires and demands that underlie those resentments, and appreciations.

Underneath are unfulfilled wishes and desires. Whenever you find yourself resenting someone, ask yourself what I'm not getting from him? And then agree to at least ask for it. As we talked earlier, the worst you'll get is no. You could just get a yes. But at least the request will be available.

Some of the most important behaviors for most people are saying the facts when it's awkward. Most of us are so concerned about hurting the feelings of others; we don't express our true feelings. We end up hurting ourselves.

• There's No "Perfect Time" To Tell the Hard Truth

There's no "right moment" to tell the hard truth knowing earlier to speak your truth is one of the most critical success behaviors you'll ever create. As soon as you ask yourself the question, I wonder when would be the best time, to tell the truth, it's probably the best time to do so.

Will it be uncomfortable? Perhaps so. Creates tons of reactions? Yeah, yeah. But it's the right thing. Stay used to saying the facts quicker. You want to get where you say it as soon as you think it. That's when you're real. What you see, you get.

People know where you're. You can count on speaking your mind.

5.4 Talk with Impeccability

Word impeccability can lead you to personal independence, great prosperity, and abundance; it can take away all anxiety and turn it into happiness and love.

Don Miguel Ruiz

For most of us, our sentences are spoken without consciousness. We never avoid worrying about what we're doing. Our ideas, views, assumptions, and beliefs roll our tongues off without concern for the harm or benefits they can bring.

Successful men, by contrast, master their expressions. I know if they don't control their thoughts, their thoughts will rule them. They are mindful of their thoughts and words — both about themselves and others. They realize they need to speak words that build self-esteem and self-confidence, build relationships, and create dreams — words of affirmation, motivation, gratitude, affection, acceptance, potential, and vision — to be more effective.

Speaking with impeccability is the highest self. It means speaking with meaning and dignity. It means your words correspond with what you think you want to produce — your vision, your dreams.

• Your Word Has Power

If you speak with impeccability, your words have an influence not only over yourself but also with others. Speaking with impeccability is saying only words true, uplifting, and affirming the importance of others.

When you learn to talk impeccably, you will find that words are the foundation of all relationships. How I talk to you, and you decide our relationship's consistency.

- What You Say to Someone Creates a Ripple Effect in the World

Successful people say words of inclusion, not words of exclusion, words of acceptance, not words of rejection, and words of compassion, not words of bigotry

When I show affection and acceptance, you'll feel love for me. If I show judgment and disdain, you'll judge me back. If I express gratitude for you, you will express gratitude and appreciation to me. When I express hate words to you, you'll most likely hate me again.

All you say produces worldwide influence. Anything you tell someone else has an impact on that person. Know that you actively construct something — positive or negative — with your words.

- Stop Lying

As with negative behavior, you not only isolate yourself from your higher self, but you also run the risk of being exposed and further eroding the confidence of others.

- Their Word Isn't Impeccable

Lying is the result of low self-esteem — belief that you and your abilities are inadequate to get what you want. It's also focused on the mistaken assumption you can't manage the implications of people learning the truth about you — which is yet another way to say I'm not enough.

When you talk ill of another to someone else, it may briefly bind you to that other person, but it creates a permanent impression on the other that you are the kind of person who negates others. The other person will still wonder — even unconsciously — when you turn the verbal poison on them. This will erode their deep faith in you.

• Check Your Thoughts and Feelings

How do you know when your word was impeccable? You feel healthy, happy, cheerful, calm, and peaceful. If you don't feel these things, test your emotions, self-talk, and verbal and written contact with others.

When you begin to be more impeccable with your term, you begin to see changes in all aspects of your life.

5.5 When in Doubt, Check It Out

So many people waste precious time and scarce resources, asking what other people are thinking, planning, or doing. Instead of asking for clarity, they make assumptions — usually thinking about themselves — and then make decisions based on those assumptions.

Productive men, on the other hand, don't waste time or wonder. They just check it out: "I wonder if ..." or "it's okay ...?" or" You feel ...?" They don't fear rejection, so inquire.

• People Always Imagine Something Worst When They Don't Know What Is True

People imagine the worst if they don't realize what's real, what's the underlying question of believing anything. Generally, people are most afraid of what they don't know. Rather of verifying items, they presume evidence that does not exist, instead of bias around such assumptions. They make poor decisions based on these assumptions, rumors, or views of others.

Consider the difference when you know all the details about a circumstance, person, question, or opportunity. Then you can make choices and take action based on what's true, rather than what you make up.

How much do you make assumptions — good or bad — without testing them? Would you believe, without testing, that both parties can produce a special project on time? By verifying that what you have is what everyone needs? Can you think at the end of a meeting that everybody is aware of who is responsible for having what action items completed by which date?

Imagine how much better not to assume — and then ask, "John, you're going to complete the study by next Friday. Okay? And marry, at five, you'll get a quote from Tuesday's printer. Okay? "Testing it out contributes to your success testing your assumptions improves your communication, relationships, quality of life, and particularly workplace performance and productivity. You see great results.

• Checking It Out Contributes to Your Success

You don't show missing pieces. You don't make assumptions on what people they didn't do. Whenever you know that Barbara won't finish on time, you call Barbara. You're testing.

How do you do when you've won? Creating a company to simply make money, accomplish some social objective, ultimately sell the company and cash out for a big profit and early retirement, use it as a political tool, solve some problem in the world? What's your goal? What are your core values? What's the escape strategy?

5.6 Uncommon Practice Appreciation

In this world, there is more desire for love and gratitude than for food.

Mother Teresa

A recent management study reported that 46 percent of workers leaving an organization do so because they feel unappreciated; 61 percent said their managers do not attach much value to them as individuals, and 88 percent said they do not receive appreciation for their work.

Whether you're an entrepreneur, boss, instructor, parent, mentor, or just a friend, you must master the art of gratitude if you want to be productive with others.

Consider each year; a management consultancy company conducts a survey of 200 businesses about what motivates workers. If offered a list of 10 potential motivational items, workers often mention gratitude as the number-one motivator. When asked to rate the same directory, the managers and supervisors ranked number eight. It's a significant mismatch, as the chart below shows so clearly.

• Three Kinds of Appreciation

Defining three different forms of recognition — auditory, visual, and kinesthetic — is essential. Those are the three main ways the brain receives information, and everyone has a dominant type they prefer.

Auditors need to understand, graphics need to see it, and kinesthetic needs to experience it.

• The Perfect Combination

When in doubt, using all three communication types — auditory, visual, and kinesthetic. Tell them, show them, and give them a back pat. You may take a person's hands in yours, look at them squarely in your eyes, and tell them honestly and expressively that you value them and their efforts. Then give the person a reminder card or gift. And you can place your arm around your son or daughter as you walk down the beach, tell your child how much you love him or her, and then follow up with a note. You're going to make your case.

• Gratitude as A Secret of Success

Another significant reason to be in a state of appreciation as much as possible is that in such a rule, you are in one of the highest possible vibrational (emotional) states. When you're in a state of love and gratitude, you're plentiful. You enjoy what you do, rather than dwell and lament about what you don't have. Your concentration is on what you've got, so you still get something to concentrate on. And as the rule of attraction says that you should draw something abundance — more to be grateful for — to you. (the more thankful you are, the more grateful you will be.) This is an upward-spiraling cycle of ever-increasing fulfillment that just keeps getting better and better. Think about it. The more grateful people we give them, the more likely we are to provide them with more presents. Their gratitude and appreciation reinforce our gift. On a social and metaphysical basis, the same concept exists as on an interpersonal level.

5.7 Protect Your Agreements

To the degree that you maintain your agreements.

Werner Erhard

Typically, one's word was one's bond. Agreements were rendered with limited fanfare. People thought twice about keeping their obligations before committing to anything. That's significant. Holding one's relationships today seems a hit-or-miss thing.

You incur external and internal costs when you don't keep your agreements. You lose faith, respect, and reputation with others — your family, friends, colleagues, and customers.

And you make messes in your own life and in the lives of others who rely on you to do things — whether it's turning up on time to leave for movies, getting a report finished on time or cleaning the garage.

After a few weeks of not keeping your pledge to take the kids to the park on weekends, they start not trusting you to hold your word. They know they can't count. Through them, you lose control. Your friendship worsens.

• Every Agreement You Make Is with Yourself
More importantly, any transaction you make with yourself is ultimate with you. Even if you agree with anyone else, the brain hears and records it as a promise. You plan to do something about yourself, and when you don't follow through, you learn to hate yourself. The consequence is self-esteem, self-confidence, and self-respect. You lose confidence in producing a product. You lose a sense of honesty.

Let's say you're asking your partner to wake up at 6:30 a.m. And do some exercise before going to work. But after three days of snooze warning, your brain knows better than trusting you. Sleeping late may not be a big deal, of course, but to your unconscious, it's a big deal. If you don't do what you're thinking, you generate uncertainty and self-doubt. You lose your power sense. It's not worthwhile.

5.8 Be A Class Act

There are "human benchmarks " − some people whose actions are a pattern for all else − shining examples that others respect and imitate. They call these individuals "class players." dan Sullivan "be a class act."

Dan Sullivan

Strive to be the kind of individual behaving with class, is known as a class act, and attracting those of course to their sphere of influence.

Today's tragic reality in society is that there don't seem to be as many groups messing around as before. All would accept that actor Jimmy Stewart was a class act. Tom Hanks' class act. Paul Newman and Denzel Washington. Coretta Scott King and nelson Mandela's former president are both class players. Herb Kelleher, the southwest airline founder, is a class act.

Yet how do you distinguish yourself in a world where most people are unconscious and "special?" the response is that you must actively strive to liberate yourself from the many doubts, concerns, and anxieties that hinder the imaginations and aspirations of the vast majority of people and function beyond the traditional world in a world of increasing knowledge, innovation, and achievement. But you need a class act behavior model to direct your thoughts and behavior.

• Why Was A Class Act Successful?

Indeed, that's one of the critical advantages of becoming a class act: people want to do business with you or get interested in your sphere of influence. They see you as good as someone who can extend their possibilities. They trust you to behave responsibly, honesty, and aplomb.

Maybe that's why showing people class acts is the best way to spot class acts.

Look at people they're doing business with, people they're socializing with. Class acts continue to draw top-of-the-game men.

Have you looked at your relatives, colleagues, partners, clients, and contacts lately? Are these individual acts? If not, find this difference as a mirror representing your standing. Decide to re-create as a class act now and see what kind of people you start attracting. Do fewer things, but do more. Raise the level of your mindset and strengthen habits.

• Class Acts Teaching Others to Treat Them with Esteem

Of course, one of the first people you should treat with respect and admiration is yourself. If you're sloppy, you're always late, and you don't care how you conduct yourself, you're going to meet people who treat you in a careless, time-consuming, care-free way.

If the head of state, the pope, or the Dalai Lama had come to visit your home, wouldn't you have house cleaners in there for a week? Wouldn't you buy some of the best food? Well, why don't you do that on your own? You're just as important as that!

The bottom line is some people have a certain level of respect not only for how they treat others but, more importantly, for how they handle themselves. When you set a higher level of personal standards, not only do you get better treatment from those around you but all of a sudden, you also begin to attract others with the same high standards. You're invited to places where these standards exist. You're going to enjoy the activities that people in the upper echelons enjoy. All of this by becoming a class act.

6

Quality and Money

There's complexity science, and it's an exact science, like algebra or arithmetic. Specific rules are regulating the process of acquiring wealth, and once someone learns and obeys these rules, that individual becomes rich with mathematical certainty.

Wallace d. Wattles

6.1 Build a Positive Money Consciousness

Like all else addressed in this book, financial success also begins in mind. You must first determine what you want. First, believe it's possible, and you deserve it. Then you have to concentrate on it, thinking about it and visualizing it as if it were yours. And then, you have to pay the price to get it — with concentrated commitment and perseverance over time.

But most people never enter the first stages of accumulating capital. Too often, they are constrained by their own belief in money and whether or not they deserve it.

• Identify Your Limiting Beliefs about Money

Recognize your limiting beliefs about money you need to surface, recognize, root out, and remove any negative or limiting conviction you might have about money. While it may seem strange that someone has a negative predisposition to money, we still keep these views in our childhood subconscious.

You may hear when you were young:

-Money doesn't grow on trees.

- Not enough money to go around.

- You need money to make profits.

- Money causes all bad.

- Money is cruel, corrupt, and immoral.

Such early childhood signals will potentially undermine and dilute your later financial success, as they subconsciously emit a vibration contrary to your conscious intentions.

What did your parents, grandparents, teachers, religious figures, peers, and colleagues tell you as you grew up and as a young adult?

You will make several restricting decisions about money that will prevent you from having or enjoying the amount of money you need.

• Using the Power of Releasing to Accelerate Your Millionaire Mind-Set

Whenever you make your money affirmations — or any affirmation, for that matter — it's not unusual to be aware of competing thoughts (objections), like who are you kidding?

You'll never be wealthy. How many times will I tell you? You need money to make it. When this occurs, first write down the complaint. Instead you can close your eyes and release the thinking and the associated emotions. Here's a quick release method, a variation of the Sedona method taught by hale doeskin.

• Visualize What You Want as If You Have It

Remember to include money in your everyday visualizations, viewing all of your financial goals as achieved. See photos showing the ideal income amount, such as paychecks, rent checks, tax checks, dividend statements, and cash handers. See examples of your bank statements, investment reports and portfolios. See photos of things you could purchase, do, and contribute if you had already achieved all your financial goals. Make sure to add kinesthetic and olfactory measurements to your visually — notice the sleek sensation of the finest silk in the world on your face, experience the relaxing feeling of a lavish massage in the world's finest spas, and the fragrance of your favorite cuts of flora that will fill your house, or your favorite imported perfume's elegant aroma. First, add the sound of the waves lapping up on the beach in front of your holiday home or the soft hum of your new Porsche's finely tuned engine.

Eventually, try to incorporate appreciation and gratitude for getting these items already. The sense of abundance is part of what draws you more abundance. Fill your mind with pictures of what you want and imagine yourself getting them.

6.2 You Get What You Focus On

If you don't place a premium on money and try wealth, you probably won't obtain it. To seek you, you must seek money.

When you have no burning need for money, no money can emerge around you. Definite reason for acquiring wealth is important for acquiring it.

Dr. John DeMartini

It's said you get what you concentrate on in life. This rule applies when finding new job, building a company, winning an award — but mostly gaining income, wealth, and a wealthy lifestyle.

• You Must Decide to Be Wealthy

One of the first aspects of being wealthy is making a deliberate decision to do so. If you want wealth, you will now decide from the deepest position in your heart to have wealth in your life — without worrying, whether possible or not.

• Next, Decide What Wealthy Means You

Know how much wealth you want? Some of my colleagues want to retire as millionaires, while others want to retire with $30m or even $100m. Two friends want to become mega-rich due to their philanthropic capacity. There's no financial target to set. But you must know what you want.

If you haven't defined your dream yet ("decide what you want") — including identifying your financial goals — take time to do so now. Do not allow your mind to convince you that these things are unlikely or insane. Only do the homework for the moment and figure out exactly what it will cost to fund your perfect life — whatever it is.

• Get Serious About Your Retirement

Determine how much you will sustain to your current lifestyle until you retire and stop working. While I don't really expect to stop working, if retirement is in your future, Charles Schwab says that for every $1,000 in monthly income you'll want during retirement, you'll need to have $230,000 saved when you quit working.

If that's enough will depend on a variety of factors, such as how your house is paid for, how many people you'll be helping, how much you will be getting from social security, and what type of lifestyle you plan to enjoy. At any pace, today $4,300 a month may not be enough to afford the lavish lifestyle you might be envisioning for yourself. If you are looking to fly and have an active life, it might not even be sufficient. With inflation, it might be less than sufficient.

• Become Conscious About Your Money

Make your money conscious most people are unaware about their money. You know, for example, your net worth—your total assets minus your total liabilities?

Do you know exactly what your monthly expenses are? Do you know how much debt you bear and how much money you spend a year on interest payments? Know if you're properly insured? You have a financial plan? Are you planning an estate? You got a will? Is it updated?

If you want to be financially efficient, be conscious. Not only do you know exactly where you are, but you do also know exactly where you want to go and what you need to get there.

• Wealth Has Several Faces

Lee Brower, the founder of empowered wealth and a member of my mastermind party, created a model for teaching people how to manage all their wealth—not only their financial wealth. If you look at the chart below, you'll see that you have four different properties.

Second, your human properties. These include your family, your fitness, your character, your special talents, your heritage, your relationships, your behaviors, and your principles, morals, and values.

Secondly, your human properties, including your expertise, abilities and schooling, your life interactions (every positive and every negative thing), your honesty, your systems, your thoughts, the values you have acquired or developed and your relationships through the years. The second is your intangible properties.

The third element is your financial properties, including capital, securities and bonds, your savings plan funds, your real estate, any business you operate or any other property you might have, such as your selection of antiquities.

The fourth are what lee calls public properties, which could include just the taxes you pay (and the programs and facilities they provide). This might even include the tax revenue that you "redirect" by donations to deserving causes, and if you are one of the super-rich, you may also have a private fund.

6.3 Pay Yourself First

You have a sacred right to wealth, and if you are anything less than a millionaire, you haven't had your fair share.

Stuart Wilde

The first idea the money lender tells Arkad is: "a part of what you earn must be yours to keep." He goes on to demonstrate that by first setting aside at least 10 percent of his earnings — and keeping that money unavailable for expenses — Arkad will see this sum accumulate over time and, in turn, start earning money on its own. In an even longer time, it will develop into a number, because of the power of compound interest.

Many people have created their fortunes by paying themselves first. It's as valid and successful today as it was in 1926.

• The Eighth Miracle of the Compound's

Foreign significance is the eighth natural wonder of the universe and the strongest element I have ever seen.

Albert Einstein

When you're fresh in compound theory, here's how it works: if you pay $1,000 at the 10% interest rate, you earn $100 in dividends and have a net gain of $1,100 by the end of the first year. If you put both your original payment and the charged interest on the portfolio, you can receive a 10% return on $1,100 next year, which is $110. You'll gain 10 percent for $1,210 in the third year – and so on as soon as you give it. At this level, your money is expected to double every seven years.

That is how it eventually turns over time into a huge number.

Naturally, the greatest news is the friend's moment when the attraction is compound. The faster you launch, the bigger the outcome.

• Make Saving and Savings A Goal

The most effective savers in the world are finding investing capital as important as paying mortgages.

To raise money every month, carry your salary directly with you and transfer it into a savings plan that you will not allow yourself to use.

Keep building your portfolio until you've invested enough to transfer it into a mutual fund or bond portfolio or to invest it in real estate — including the purchase of your own house. The amount of money that is spent paying rent without building any equity in a home is a tragedy for many people.

If you just spend 10% to 15% of your earnings, you will eventually create a wealth. First pay yourself, then live on what remains. It will do two things: (1) it would push you to develop a wealth and (2) it will cause you to find opportunities to earn more capital so you can spend more or do something.

Never use your money to help your greater lifestyle. You want your savings to rise to the point that, if necessary, you can live off value. Only then would you be absolutely financially secure.

• The 50/50 Law

Another law that John recommends is that you never pay more than you receive. John saves 50 cents of every dollar he receives. If he decides to increase his personal expenses by $45,000, he will first raise another $90,000. Let's say you want a $40,000 car. If you can't save $40,000 more, you don't buy the car. Either buy a cheaper car, do what's right now, or go out and make more money. The trick is that you don't increase your spending unless you earn the right to increase it by saving the same amount. If you increase your savings by $40,000, you know you've raised the same amount to boost your lifestyle.

The 50/50 law quickly makes you rich. It was the foundation of sir john marks Templeton's wealth-building strategy.

• How to Become an "Automatic Millionaire"?

The easiest way to execute the first program pay is to have a program that is completely "free " — that is, set up to automatically subtract and spend a percentage of your paycheck as you guide.

Financial planners will inform you, from their vast experience with hundreds of clients, that very few — if any — follow a strategy to pay themselves first, if not immediately. When you're an employee, search with your employer about self-directed retirement accounts such as 401(k) plans.

You can allow the business to automatically subtract your donation from your paycheck. If deducted before collecting your receipt, you'll never miss it. More significantly, you won't have to worry about your investments — you won't have to be self-disciplined. It's not about the mood swings, family crises, or anything else. You make the effort once and it's over. Another advantage of these plans is that they are most tax-free before you withdraw the money. And, instead of 70 cents working for you, you've got a whole dollar working for you — compounding year after year.

Some organizations would also suit your donation. If you're working for such a service, join now! Check the company's employee benefits office to find out how to sign up. When you do, make sure you make the largest contribution by statute, but at least 10%. When you can't get yourself to do 10 percent, do the biggest amount you can. Reassess and see if you can't raise it after a few months. Get imaginative on where to cut costs and how to increase your income from some other source.

When you don't have a retirement plan, you can open an individual retirement account (IRA) at a bank or brokerage. You make up to $3,000 a year for an IRA ($3,500 if you're 50 or older). Ask the bank, brokerage or financial planner to help you determine whether you want a standard IRA or a Roth IRA. Starting an IRA takes around the same time as opening a checking account. And you should pay to automatically subtract it from your bank account.

• Create Assets over Liabilities

Rule one. You must know the Terence dive between asset and responsibility and buy assets. Poor and middle-class take on liabilities, however they believe they're properties. An asset that puts money in my wallet. A liability is something my pocket takes money.

So many people waste and whim their financial lives. For most people, this is their "investment" model:

But look at how rich people handle their investments. They take the money they raise and spend all of it in income-producing assets — real estate, small companies, stocks, shares, gold, etc. To become rich, follow their lead. Start your financial activities like this:

• Protect What Is Yours with Insurance

It's a sad fact today that many affluent people are targets of baseless litigation, accusations, and other complaints—often for no good cause. Additionally, errors and injuries will still occur, so protecting your financial assets through a good insurance policy is crucial. That's even more important if you're a small business.

Locate a good insurance broker like you'd consider a financial advisor or wealth management service.

• Save What's Yours with A Prenuptial or Cohabitation Agreement

When you get married later in life or bring several assets to the union, most financial experts will advise you to sign a prenuptial agreement. I know it may sound like you're adding a negative matter to an experience that should be one of love and happiness, but these days it's almost become a necessity. I've seen so many people—both men and women—loose what was rightfully theirs because they were afraid to get a prenuptial agreement.

When you can't speak freely about a prenuptial arrangement, as they occur, you probably won't be able to speak freely about other complicated emotional issues. This doesn't bode well for relationship success or longevity. Find a decent marriage counselor and a few decent lawyers—whose prenuptial arrangements have held up in court—and hammer out a compromise you can feel good about. To you both, it can be a really clarifying personal development experience.

6.4 Master the Spending Game

Spending master too many people waste money they haven't earned, buy stuff they don't want, please people they don't want.

Will Rogers

Will Rogers how much spent last year?

Spending too much can harm your financial goals. It holds you in debt, prevents you from investing as much as you can, and turns your attention to consumption rather than accumulation of capital.

If you are unable to curtail spending, try this exercise. Go through every wardrobe, box, and cabinet in your house and take out everything you haven't used in the past year. This includes clothing, shoes, jewelry, utensils, furniture, sheets, towels, blankets, sporting equipment, audiocassettes, CDs, films, games, toys, auto accessories, and tools—anything and all you spent money on but didn't use in the last year. Gather everything in one location, like your living room, dining room or workshop. Instead sum up the amount per everything you pay. I encountered people who found expensive clothes with tags still attached, housewares bags never unboxed, and costly devices and equipment used only once, maybe 3 or 4 years earlier.

The fact is that with the exception of tuxedos, evening gowns, ski boots, and snorkel equipment you may use just once every few years, you actually never really needed all those items in the first place.

Yet you spent money on them. So, when you add up what these things cost, you can notice the amount would be more than your existing credit card debt.

Start Charging Money for Virtually Everything

One way to minimize inflation is to start charging money for everything. Money is more urgent. It lets you think of what you're buying. You'll also find yourself spending less than you would if you used credit cards. Every future expenditure will be considered more carefully, "essential" incidentals will become less important, and major transactions will possibly be put off, forcing you to think about whether you can make do without them.

• Reduce the Expense of Your Wealthy Lifestyle

Another way to conquer the spending game is to live the lifestyle you want and pay a whole lot less for it.

Some people barter for products and services, press for discounts even when they're not offered, press if they can purchase the item cheaper, call four or five vendors and take bids for the same similar item, regularly suck every dollar they can out of the cost of living the lavish lifestyle they want.

For these people—who are all militant savers—living this kind of lifestyle on as little money as possible is almost like a challenge.

• Take Action now to Become Debt Free

Another big part of winning the spending game is to actually get out of debt. Avoid charging high credit card interest rates and expect a less consumptive lifestyle.

It's incredible that as a country, we've accrued as much personal debt as we have. Credit card, mortgage, and auto fees are overwhelming for many individuals. Savings and financial stability fail. If this is your case, take action now to start living life debt free.

• The Power of Focus

As you commit to being debt free and saving more, you'll experience an almost magical force operating in your life. As you change your attention from investing and consuming to loving the stuff you already have and setting money aside, you'll advance at an almost unexplainable pace.

Also, if you don't believe you'll succeed every month, once you commit to a debt-reduction and savings program, you'll be shocked at your ability to handle and arrive at your target quicker than you had expected.

You can go through a profound transformation. You'll see your beliefs and goals change.

Suddenly, you'll calculate your performance in terms of debts paid off rather than goods bought. And as your investment portfolio increases, you'll begin to balance all investments against your goal to be financially stable and debt free.

6.5 Invest More, First Make More

Whatever can be said in praise of poverty, the truth remains that leading a truly full or productive life is impossible unless one is wealthy.

Wallace d. Wattles

Basically, there are only two ways to end up with more investment capital or extra luxuries — either spending less money first, or actually making it. Personally, I'm a fan of more. I'd rather invest more than constantly deny myself stuff I want for some distant future benefit.

The truth is that having more money means you can both save more and spend more on the stuff you want — travel, clothes, art, concerts, fine food, quality medical care, world-class entertainment experiences, premium transportation, schooling, hobbies, and all kinds of time- and labor-saving tools and services.

The first move in making more money is to decide how much more you want to produce. We spoke extensively about utilizing the power of encouragement and visualization to see the wealth. Not unexpectedly, the planet has history after history of the super-rich, who have used such daily activities to make their lives more money.

The second step is to ask what good, service or value-added can I provide for that money? What do you need on the world, your supervisor, your buddies, your company partners, your coworkers or your clients?

Finally, the third stage is to create and deliver the product, service or added value.

More Money Ideas

1: Become an Entrepreneur

Today, many of America's smartest businesses foster entrepreneurship among their workers and executives. If one of these businesses is your employer, or if you can persuade your manager to give you a share of the new money you raise from ignored revenue areas, you can increase your income almost immediately.

Maybe the employer's client list is not offering additional products and services. Perhaps the workgroup is so good at running tasks, its leaders have free time to "employ" other teams for extra pay.

Maybe there's a piece of equipment, a vendor arrangement, an ignored marketing strategy, or some uncommon commodity the employer doesn't make full use of. You may build a strategy to turn this asset into cash, and approach your employer with a proposal to work on the asset-maximizing off-hours project for extra pay. You might also get a well-deserved promotion.

2: First Find a Need and Fill It Accordingly

I've never mastered an innovation I didn't think about in terms of value it might offer others. I figure out what the world wants, so I invent.

Thomas a. Edison

Some of the most successful people in history have recognized a need in the marketplace and given a solution to it, but most of them never questioned what was needed — or even what was possible.

If your vision is to raise more money — either through your own company or in addition to your job — identify an unmet need and decide how to fulfill it.

Whether it's launching a website for a specific community of enthusiasts, offering a unique education for people who need special or uncommon skills, or designing new products or services to tackle emerging trends you see in society beside this there are always needs you can identify to build a company or service around them.

Some of these former needs are technologies and programs we take for granted now. But the truth remains that people found what they wanted in their own lives or stumbled on others' needs, then developed the products and services we enjoy today.

Demand is practically everywhere. If you're a college student searching for a summer income, a housewife trying to raise an additional $500 a month to make ends meet, or an entrepreneur searching for the next big business opportunity — there's still a need to make some serious money.

The possibilities are limitless do you see a similar need in life? What about the desire or ambition of those around you? Is there anything to have, fix, tackle, or eliminate? Is there anything you find irritating that could be alleviated if there were some tool or service to solve the problem? Share a shared purpose or dream with someone in your business or social circle you could accomplish if only someone gave you a method or mechanism to accomplish it? Do you enjoy those things that make a new product or service even more enjoyable?

Look at your own life and wonder what's missing, making things simpler or satisfying.

As an income generation expert, Janet Switzer works with countless internet entrepreneurs, helping them raise more money from their online businesses. Today, an internet company is one of the easiest to start and operate — even while holding your work. You can find and satisfy a need for a very small market, and touch thousands and even millions of people worldwide with that need.

You can also sell downloadable e-books, audio files, apps, training materials, special reports, how-to courses, and other information products — meaning you never have to send a single box or envelope. Many products are also easy to market, of course. It's all about figuring out who needs what, how best to meet them, and how to persuade them to buy.

The good news is the internet is a permanent marketplace. Hundreds of other blogs, newsletters, and clubs also have guests, subscribers, and members who would be ideal prospective customers for you if you give another website owner or affiliate a percentage. One Janet's client modeled this affiliate program and received 578,667 new visitors to his website in just 90 days. Many of those people continuously purchased goods and services from website creator.

When you know how to market online, you can also market the goods of other people online. A Florida man approached his local jeweler and asked him if he ever thought of selling his jewelry online. The jeweler answered he had thought about it, but never had the time to get around to do it. He agreed to build the website and push traffic for a percentage of income. The jeweler agreed readily. This was a win-win for both.

#3: Enter a Network Marketing Company

There are more than 1,000 businesses offering their goods and services through network marketing — surely one or more are excited about. From health products to food, cookware, toys, educational materials, and telecommunications services — even low-cost legal and financial services — there's something for everyone. A little internet work can yield many opportunities.

Since many network marketing firms don't last, make sure you get sound advice before you get involved. Find a business that's been around for a while, with a strong reputation. Try them and make sure you enjoy them. If you're passionate about the product and passionate about people, you can make a lot of money through the leverage given by building down line. Very few companies can capitalize on such a massive opportunity with such a small financial investment.

Wherever you decide to place your money, the goal is to make your current employer, clients, or consumers more valuable. You do this by better addressing their issues, providing goods, and integrating resources they want and need.

You can need more experience, new skills, more relationships, or extra time. Yet it's your duty to get better at what you do and how you do it.

Find opportunities for further preparation and self-development. If you need an advanced degree or credential to step up in your chosen trade or career, stop talking and go get it.

Create Multiple Income Sources

The best way to experience higher income and build economic stability in your life is to establish multiple income sources. This protects you from any of those sources — usually your job — drying and leaving you without cash flow.

A Significant Distinction

When creating multiple sources of income, do your best to concentrate on starting and running companies that need very little time and energy. Your main aim is to set it up so you're free to work anywhere you want — or take time off to enjoy leisure. Too many fragmented sources mean you risk losing your key source of income.

6.6 Give More to Get More

Offer more to bring all the tenths in the storehouse to feed in my house to place me to task, says the Lord of hosts, before I open for you the windows of the heavens, and spill down an overflowing blessing.

Tithing — that is, to give the work of God 10 percent of your earnings — is one of the greatest promises of redemption. Many of the wealthiest men in the world and most powerful individuals have been dedicated dithers. Every year, you too will trigger God's spiritual force, granting you continuous abundance.

This not only serves everyone; it also serves you as the giver. The benefits cross all religious lines and represent people of every faith — because the simple act of giving establishes both a spiritual bond with the abundant god and fosters the mind-set of caring for others. Tithing proves compellingly that god desires ample riches for his children. Yes, the more successful you become, the more money there is for us to share. Growing an individual's wealth almost always represents an increase in society's wealth.

• Specific Tithing Methods

There are two different types of tithing. Financial tithing is best described as donating 10% of your gross income to the entity from which you receive your spiritual guidance or support your philanthropic work.

Time tithing is donating your time to support the church, temple, or synagogue, or any charity that might benefit. About 18,000 charities in the United States alone currently need volunteers.

• Corporate Giving

Corporations, too, will enjoy the return bonuses. William h. George, Medtronic's chairman and CEO, recently disclosed to a Minneapolis conference on philanthropy how his organization had committed to giving 2% of their pre-tax income. While at the beginning these "titles" amounted to just $1.5 million, the 11-year growth streak of 23 percent a year allowed them to raise their $17 million in one year alone.

Perhaps the most remarkable recent acts of giving were ted turner's $1 billion donation to the un and bill and Melinda gates' $7 billion grants through the bill and Melinda gates foundation. You don't have to be a company or super rich to give the society back. Any donation, whether in time or money, will make a difference to the recipients and to you, both in the positive feelings you will encounter and in the increased flow of abundance into your life.

• Sharing Wealth

Money's like manure. If you spread it around it, it's fine. But if you pile it in one spot, it's like hell.

Junior Murchison

When you engage others in your success — when you share the wealth with them — more work is completed, more success is accomplished, and eventually all gain more.

Conclusion

Success is the most desired feeling that we all want to experience in the pursuit of our goals and also in our daily lives. Each individual has his or her definition of success. If you're going to succeed in your life or as a business owner, you need to be able to focus.

In order to excel, it is crucial to consider at the moment what is essential, identify and focus on flaws, critique and maintain strengths. From a wider view, performance determines joy, peace of mind and pure pleasure. One can note that it can only be effective through perseverance.

Successful sustainable business practices often require entrepreneurship and innovation. This book provides an overview of the fundamentals of success, entrepreneurship, and change about sustainable business. Discussion is most relevant to the different strategies and principles that focus on delivering success in your life and business.

Taking your life and your business to another level of success doesn't have to be such a traumatic experience. It might be a bit difficult at first, but then, once you get a grip on what you're expected to do, you'll be on the road to great success.

Once you have achieved your goals, you can be a healthy inspiration to others. There's a warrior in you, and you never shut him down. You're capable of climbing higher and booming into a fantastic personality. No matter what, live a humble life, spread positivity, and take the torch to others' path to success by making these tremendous principles a part of your life.

References

- 7 Storytelling Techniques and How To Apply Them | Practical Ecommerce. Practical Ecommerce. Retrieved from **https://www.practicalecommerce.com/7-Storytelling-Techniques-and-How-To-Apply-Them**.

- Risk attitudes are context-specific | VOX, CEPR Policy Portal. Voxeu.org. Retrieved from **https://voxeu.org/article/risk-attitudes-are-context-specific**.

- Cultural Cognition as a Conception of the Cultural Theory of Risk.

- Flaxseed oil intake reduces serum small dense low-density lipoprotein concentrations in Japanese men: a randomized, double blind, crossover study.

- Entrepreneurial Growth: An Entrepreneur's Choice. Timreview.ca. Retrieved from **https://timreview.ca/article/357**.

- Business Exit Reasons and Strategies. StartupDecisions. Retrieved from **https://www.startupdecisions.com.sg/startups/exit-planning/business-exit-strategies/**.

- Effects of Risk Attitude and Controllability Assumption on Risk Ratings: Observational Study on International Construction Project Risk Assessment.

- University Students and their faculty: Perceptions of entrepreneurial optimism, overconfidence and entrepreneurial Intentions, 20(1), 123-134. **https://doi.org/10.7202/1045360ar**

- https://www.app.pan.pl/article/item/app20120056.html. **https://doi.org/10.4202/app.2012.0056**

- 10 Things You Must Do to Be Successful in Business (and in Life). Inc.com. Retrieved from **https://www.inc.com/john-rampton/how-to-be-successful-in-business-and-be-successful-in-life-too.html**.

- Automatic Negative Thoughts (ANTs): How to Break the Habit | Be Brain Fit. Bebrainfit.com. Retrieved from **https://bebrainfit.com/automatic-negative-thoughts/**.

- What is PET Power/Smashing ANTs™. Smashingants.com. Retrieved from **https://www.smashingants.com/what-is-smashing-ants/**.

- Relationship Building in Business - Play Nice in the Sandbox with Penny Tremblay. Play Nice in the Sandbox with Penny Tremblay. Retrieved from **https://pennytremblay.com/relationships-are-key/**.

- Habits For Building Client Relationship - FLEXcon. Flexcon.com. Retrieved from **https://www.flexcon.com/industry-insights/relationships/habits-for-building-client-relationship**.

- Taming Your Inner Critic: 7 Steps To Silencing The Negativity. Forbes. Retrieved from **https://www.forbes.com/sites/amymorin/2014/11/06/taming-your-inner-critic-7-steps-to-silencing-the-negativity/#1a5b06837feb**.

www.ingramcontent.com/pod-product-compliance
Lightning Source LLC
Chambersburg PA
CBHW030947240526
45463CB00016B/2041